water. pistol.

Younger Charles Robbins

ADJAR

Published by Adjar, LLC 2022
Younger Robbins: Member Adjar, LLC
Logo design: Erin Cathcart

Cover art by:
Chris Mott
@chrismottart

ISBN: 978-0-578-88782-1

Thank You

2015 Los Angeles, CA

...I boned it up pretty good by now. I don't know if you'll be able to see a way through it. I was hoping this voice memo would help... but now that I've started, I'm not sure I'll be able to remember the end. Something like Fred MacMurray in the Billy Wilder movie about insurance sales: good old Fred, hanging around the same Sunset lights as Holden. Writer and underwriter, victims of their trades. My phone's dying, and this guy only has a fuckin' Android charger in his desk, so I'll make it quick. I never should have come to California... let Randy Newman have Venice beach. I'll take Revere at 10° below in fuckin' January.

If I light a cig will smoke come out my gut like the cat in those cartoons when he gets shot up by the mouse... Scratchy, not Tom. What the hell do I know about natural springs? Leave that shit to the big dogs. Big dogs eat first and last. That's what a friend told me... a friend of yours. Does Mass Health cover transportation of the deceased? Don't let them bury me in this fuckin' desert. Bury me beside the old North Church... give me roses in my garden bower, dig.

I managed to get a cig and light it with one hand... no smoke holes down there, more blood... it's turning black. I think that means it's in my stomach, which means all that stomach stuff can pour out into my like, body cavity... bad news from there. The expectorant on my mouth is bright lipstick. I like this shade and how it sticks to the filter of the cig... *Jo Burke: #09–With a Bullet.*

Thin white creases from the cracks in my lips. It's only available for a limited time. About nine pints is all before the line gets discontinued... out of stock...

Have you ever been back east? Not Lorring up in bumfuck Caribou or Kittery or wherever you got ejaculated out of to go smear the Pacific all over itself with a .60CAL and a Catholic Prayer... before you ever realized that your fellow man killed and died an awful lot like you. Joined the combat medics and got yourself shot. Came home and fell in with beat before anyone called it anything and found yourself in Northern California attending non-violent protests that consisted of like, smoking opium in the back of some theatre and making derisive comments over the newsreel. Or booing at Charles Lindbergh rallies before finally getting your shit together enough to settle down in San Jose with a little news editor gig: wife, kiddo, two-car garage. And hey, I don't judge you... especially not now, I sure as hell don't.

I had a safe little job a few days ago. They probably erased my employee number after three no call-no shows. Probably cut the lock off my locker and tossed my apron and a half bag of Parmesan Goldfish, and like, two loose cigs and about 10 empty packs of Marlboro Lights, and a little emergency grass and a one-hitter in a make-up bag which consisted of like, some blush and a bunch of brushes off the shelf. And if you looked hard enough, you'd see that though there were plenty of receipts in the bottom of the locker, very few of them detailed the purchase of any of those things.

You could have come and seen me some time. We'd go see a game at the Garden... shoot putt-putt through the T-Rex on the way to get a steak at Frank Giuffrida's. It isn't exactly Cambridge, but who the fuck wants to live in Cambridge anyway? This is where my Mother's family finally settled after drag-assing all across the country from base to base at the call of the then much revered—even by those who thought themselves semi-informed—US Military Complex's varying job market at home and abroad. Making something like a living, careering from one public school to another in a station wagon with probably not as many worldly possessions as you might imagine for a family with four teenage daughters. I wouldn't meet the man behind the wheel. Thanks to a formidable diet consisting of unfiltered Pall Malls, the classic Mickey D's #2 value meal, and a half a case of Old Milwaukee on the nightly, he joined the ranks of the working man's dead earlier than some. Mainly said to have had a good run at a time when modern medicine hadn't progressed much past nitroglycerin tablets for your first coronary and a cedar box for the second.

I never drag-assed myself out of town much further than the four years I spent at UNH studying broadcast journalism, which left me with a degree in accumulating debt and the experiences necessary to like, manage the Saugus: Parks and Rec youth soccer team. That lasted about two summers before I decided driving to Boston weekly interviewing for freelance gigs interviewing toothless Bruins who hadn't even taken off their skates wasn't what I had in mind when I initially set out to parlay higher education into a six-figure, sit on a stool and spin, on-camera personality career.

1974 San Francisco, CA

The hill is at an angle so that if you crank the seat back far enough, it's like you're lying against the edge of the world. Joe Burke has reclined his seat in such a way and, by scooching back a little, managed to get his toes off the floorboard up into that void behind the pedals.

Pedestrians walking by don't seem to notice him in that, not noticing anything but noticing everything, shoelace examining, North American, major metropolitan, no-time sort of way that suits him just fine. If this was going to take longer, he'd kick his shoes off and spread his toes. Coffee. Sandwich. The paper. A nip or three. A fifth or so. More than a pack of Marlboro Lights right down to the cotton.

Aside from the Jimmy Cagney, *top o' the world now, Ma* view, the best part of coming up to the Russian Hill summit is that the Bruins/Flyers game is coming in crystal clear despite the gloomy refraction that makes this place more of an island than the water of the bay. Gene Hart rattles off names through an earpiece that runs to a battery-operated radio propped up on the dash: Esposito—

Orr–Bucyk. Around 14 minutes into the first period, a kid named DuPont fires a shot past Gilbert, which might not have been on-net if MacLeish hadn't tipped it with the back of his stick, putting the Flyers up 1-0. But this was only the beginning.

The Golden Seals are a good enough substitute–always on Channel 44–with an endearing history as a local Bay Area team before the '67 expansion. But nothing compared to the games Burke remembered at the Garden with his father when he was a kid, before ever cracking the seal on his first bottle of the good stuff. He'd still listen to some of the Bruins regular season. Catch every game if they made it to the finals.

Another earpiece runs to a device resembling the first but with a cassette tape whirring inside the deck compartment.

RECORD and PLAY–both depressed.

A copper wire tendril from where the antenna should be to compensate for interference, distortion.

The scene playing out in the one-room apartment upstairs is easy to be distracted from. Joe's never seen it but thinks he could recreate it if given access to the necessary components. Each varying mildly within a given set of parameters: acrylic, polyester, shag, veneer, plastic in goddamn everything; all arranged in some angular array. Line of television sight shown precedent above: windows, artwork, others.

"Single income household? Government benefits? Five-year plan? 30-year plan? Savings? Retirement? History of disease, illness, heart condition? Smoker? Good for you. Nursing? Fatigued? Exhausted? Wrung out? Depressed? Perfectly normal. Time for a feeding? Hold on now, Dad. Can you boil us a cup of water? Boil it, then let it cool. Ever consider using formula? Victoria Miller, Vicky if it pleases you."

From out of her bag comes a fresh canister of *Good Start*.

"I know what you think she says," allaying fears from under her pointed nurse's cap. The starched white smock, white skirt below the knees, white stockings above the knees. Battery operated transmitter taped to the inside of her thigh. Microphone affixed behind the name badge on her lapel:

HELLO my name is:
VICTORIA
your loving Mothercraft Nurse

In his mind's eye, Joe still envisions her all hot-shit attitude and rosy cheeks. As if it was last summer they met—that she appeared to him was more like it—polishing counters at her old man's 10-stool diner in, you-don't-know-where New Hampshire.

At 60, Vicky was a testament to human health. Maintaining the hot-shit attitude, seasoned with experience, glowing from motherhood now over 20 years in her past. She made Joe look like shit with his thinning white hair, stringy arms, and that much-feared old man paunch that never seemed to go away regardless of having or not having beer or butter or even bread for Christ's sake. To him, she was perfection, the same as when she first came to him and found him again and again as time went on. Matters of opinion aside, she was the perfect candidate for a modern door-to-door wet nurse, providing expertly contrived infant rearing advice and services in addition to hawking baby formula to the growing lower-middle-class.

"You know that breastfeeding is the most beneficial way to get all the nutrients your baby needs. Do you also know that Good Start formula has all the same nutrients your baby needs plus added vitamins and minerals to support digestion, build Iron, and not to mention, give mama a well-deserved break?"

"I'm not sure we can afford to."

"Why don't you keep this canister? I was going to open it."

"We couldn't take any charity."

"Don't think of it that way. Call it a gift, from Nestlé and from me. We know how hard it is. I've been through it myself, dear. I only wish I had something at the time to help when I would get overwhelmed. I have a feeling once you see the results in your baby and in yourself, you'll want to use Good Start all the time."

"If you're sure."

"I am, dear. How's that water coming, Dad! He does know how to boil water, doesn't he?"

The women laugh. Dad shouts something fatherly.

Joe doesn't have to listen to the banter. He's not much more than quality control at this point. Making sure the sound is passable and that the tape doesn't run out. The Philly crowd roars in the right-side earpiece. The sun has almost set. Evening coolness slips in. Pedestrian traffic outnumbers the cars, all unheard.

A hit-piece published in *New Internationalist* the previous year opened the eyes of the world to conditions they were lucky enough to not have to consider regularly. But it was the brutal, *War on Want*, shit-storm from a couple months ago—controversially dubbed *The Baby Killer*—that blew the weather vane off the whole thing. It was terrible what Nestlé had been doing. No worse than others, but they were the ones coming under investigation; pushed harder than their competitors in the underdeveloped areas of African countries. Ad campaigns and info-peddlers supporting baby formula as a guarantee for healthy infants. Never mind the latrine by the river, the pump downstream. Maybe it was because of the company's history in water manufacturing that the public cried out so loud. Whatever the reason, the people wanted blood—no longer willing to settle for water—and Nestlé was the chosen lamb of big business this year to be skewered on the pike of social conscientiousness.

End of the first period. Still: Flyers 1-0. Vicky is wrapping it up in the apartment, saying her good-byes, promising to check in soon, and leaving a number for Mom and Dad to get in touch with the Mother Craft headquarters at any time. She also leaves a mail-in form to place an order for more of that life-changing Good Start formula—act now and receive a bottle, nipples, and mixer.

The broadcast heads to commercial as Joe wraps up the radio with the earpiece. He stops the tape on the sound of footsteps clacking down the hall from the closed apartment door. The tape he labels: Mulgrue. Nancy/Scott. 5/19/74, then inserts into a case made for storing cassette tapes, which already contains several dozen labeled and logged previous recordings. The electronics go under the back seat.

He cranks the Datsun awake when Vicky emerges from the glass double doors of an apartment complex across the street. He bangs the coupe around across traffic. The front tire squelches against the curb. Vicky yanks open the door and plops herself down into the passenger seat.

"Hellooo, nurse." Joe raises his eyebrows.

Vicky tosses the hat in the back seat, lets her hair down.

"How many more times we gonna do this, Joe?"

The Datsun peels into the flow of traffic without a blinker.

"We can cut and run whenever you want. Say the word."

"You know that's not what I mean."

"Class action takes time."

She throws her tote bag in the back. Rips off the hat and smock, replacing them with a light cardigan. The skirt stays on. She's gone from on-duty nurse to something resembling a letterman's girlfriend.

"Every time is worse than the last. You should have seen it."

"It never sounds too bad."

"I said seen, pal. You haven't seen it. I have to look these people in the eyes. They can't afford milk for the coffee, never mind a newborn, never mind formula."

"Bring a copy of *Want* if you're trying to educate them."

"You don't think Mother Craft would call that a conflict of interest?"

"It slips out of your bag. They find it after you leave. They might read it."

"Who has time to read? Nancy's already going back to work. Scott's been pulling overtime since her second trimester. They look like ghosts. The baby doesn't seem much better."

What's he supposed to say? Rent for a crummy apartment has skyrocketed. Childcare, a luxury. Kindergarten, even pre-school, costly. Time-consuming. Not a guarantee.

"We've got a lot of tape," he tells her, "hours. You've done good. If we turn everything over now, I'll sort out a way to hold onto the retainer plus a little extra."

"No."

"Don't you miss Boston?"

"Only what we left behind."

"There's nothing stopping us from going home."

"But we can't have him back."

"At least we'd be close."

"And get to see him buying a cup of coffee on his way to work if I waited outside DUNKIN's every morning for a week? Telling myself not to pretend to accidentally drop my purse so he has to help me pick it up and I can brush against his hand... wonder if he can tell it's me from the touch. Wouldn't you know your mother's touch?"

Joe lets a hand off the wheel, reaching out to hold hers. She lets him, even squeezes back, but he can tell by the way she examines the traffic through the laminate, there's no answer he could give that will put her at ease.

"Forget it for now, Angel. How 'bout we go get a drink?"

"I'm no angel, mister."

"Then who's that always on my shoulder?"

Vicky smiles for him, faint but real. She had always been some kind of protector to him, bailing his ass out of the fire more than once in their day. She was right, he knew, that she was no angel. Joe didn't believe in them anyway. But if not his guardian, what was the feeling lurking over his shoulder that lately, he couldn't shake. The fluttering wings that would bring his hand to the back of his neck on the most still afternoons. The reason he turned the lights on in the next room when he was sure he was alone. The reason he didn't hear what it was she said when she agreed they could both use a drink, kept drawing his gaze to the rearview instead of the road ahead.

2015 Saugus, MA

I'd been at the store about six years on-and-off, small-time in the world of mainstay grocery chains. After five years, you're looking at a pension fund that'll pay out pretty good if you can make it 40 more, and as long as we don't leap forward to some like, Morlok-over-human, regressed evolution, messed up food chain type shit, the food sales industry doesn't seem to be going anywhere. So it's an option, at least.

My store's this Stop & Shop right off Route-1 in Saugus. A night started around 11:00PM, when the last of those with truly no other place to be, shuffle to the check-stand with an entire cart full of 79¢ butt wipes, determined to push the cashier into overtime with no shortage of coupons and banana-box proclamations that the cost of type-2 diabetes treatment and low-sodium honey ham was a lot more reasonable before we started letting China push us around. Paying with a SNAP card that doesn't swipe after the third try and has to be entered manually by the cashier who doesn't mention the several packages of Nathan's: All Beef Uncured emerging from the cramped lining of this valued customer's parka.

The cashier does like, truly overlook a 24pack water under the motorized shopping cart basket, which all the butt-wipes have been loaded back into. The water's the store brand, pretty much accounted for to be lost on a multiple time per day basis. You don't even have to order the stuff. The computer has the minimum set at like, a hundred, so pretty much as soon as one's being sold it's being ordered again from one of the Raiders of the Lost Ark style warehouses that service Best Buy and Amazon and Target and all similar purveyors of good shit cheap.

There's ways to stop loss like this. Lane Hawk has sensors scanning the bottom of your basket, your Adidas, compression socks. Thermostats gauge occupancy, flow, and trends. More cameras than Foxwoods. Sensors in the deli cases monitoring not only temperature but like, volume... orientation. Next time you pick up that $14 dollar hunk of Jarlsberg and throw it back on top of the Kraft Singles—opting for good old fashioned American annatto on your grilled cheese—think of me getting a call while I'm like, wiping my ass or trying to get laid or trying to get some sleep for Christ's sake and I got this recording telling me there's a temperature discrepancy in unit A9 and to please press one to accept and pretty much not being able to roll my eyes hard enough to convey the disdain I have for that cheese, sitting or lying there with the glass of my phone pressed to my cheek trying to wipe or fuck or probably not fall back asleep and end up smoking a half a pack of smokes and having to get dressed and leave in time to hit Cumby's on my way to work.

I suppose the first, most obvious line of defense—aside from like, a more ethically responsible consumer—is an attentive and invested cashier. Vigilantly watch-dogging your order while methodically processing items, coupons, and payments at a no less than 28IPM productivity rate. Maintaining a smiley-faced air of the utmost interest in your very personal matters not usually restricted to groceries.

Us sea-coasters don't really do attentive, invested, interested, smiley-faced, and don't hold fuckin' many airs at all. Picture your most tough shit, Panorama City: Jon's Market—where you wouldn't even be in there if Vallarta was still open that late. Picture the most like, dejected, one-armed, no hobbies--not even video-games-- sacks of meat working the check-stand there and you got yourself a shining credit to humanity compared to the tight-lipped, go fuck yasself sideways muthafuckah, attitude held by employees and customers alike up and down Saugus Route-1.

Another way to account for and protect against loss is what I'm doing right now.

"This muthafuckin' piece of shit. You got a signal?" Dwayne shouts at me from like, two feet away. He's jabbing at the display of a handheld RF scanning gun.

"Nah."

"Every Goddamn night! How'm I supposed to do this shit then? Connecting to in-store processor my ass. If I ever see that processor, I'm gonna throw it out a window like that Indian muthafucka' with that water fountain."

I laugh kind of... but it's barely a joke. Dwayne's huge, with those big guy arms that look like they could be all fat, but you wouldn't want to see it come swinging at you. He probably couldn't manage to get one of the six-foot-something data processors out of its cage and through a window. Maybe if he ran into the IT guy.

"The Chief," I tell him.

"I ain't coming in tomorrow. I'll tell you that. Inventory my ass. I'm spending Saturday night with my wife."

"Fuckin'A."

"Don't fuckin'A me, Burke. You'd be right here if Mr. Jones said. Yes, boss. Time for the inventory, boss. Eatin' the shit, boss. Mmmm good. We carry this brand of shit, boss?"

"If we did, you'd be the face on the bottle."

"Goddamn right, I would. I'd be packing up my bags and my wife and going to Tahiti or wherever it is some rich ass bottled shit slinging muthafucka' summers nowadays."

"Iceland," I suggest.

"That the cold one?"

"I think they both are."

"Fuck that then. Get enough of that cold shit right here, eight outta twelve–"

A 35 thousand square-foot doorbell rings, signifying the arrival of a truck backed up to one of the receiving doors. Dwayne tosses the malfunctioning gun to the floor. It bounces twice before settling against a carton of soy sauce he was unboxing. He's already reached a phone attached to a pillar at the opposite end of the aisle.

"Night crew to the back room."

His voice rivals the bell over the intercom.

Dwayne. Good guy. A little older than me, I think. He's got a wife, no kids. They hang out on Saturdays. He wants to go to Tahiti. Been here about twice as long as me. The apron we're supposed to wear fits him like a lobster bib, so he never wears it, even if that means catching hell like, every other night from upstairs. I don't know much else about him. Most of the guys here it's a similar story. An athletic thing that didn't pan out, a college thing that didn't pan out, military, banged out a kid at eighteen and got the first job they could find. Probate, rehab, recovery, using, maintaining, slipping... it's usually better not to ask. Everybody's gotta eat.

What I'm supposed to be doing is making a mental assumption of how many cases of the store brand water I'm supposed to have on hand and decide if it's a reasonable amount to write off as loss at the end of the period. Some get lifted, some get damaged. They crack a few open and put them in the break room, some could even still be at the warehouse, and I'll get them added to an order next week. Wherever the hell they are, it ain't here, and they get balanced out.

Most of the big guys: Poland Springs, Dasani, Arrowhead, Nestlé, they deal through third-party vendors who make it their business to know how many of what's moving when and how. They show up in the middle of the night, drop 10 pallets of Coke and disappear, not my problem. My problem is, when I go to update my balance, I get an error:

ITEM CANNOT BE ORDERED BY CAO

That's the computer trying to tell me this water like, isn't mine. I don't have much in the world, but one thing I sure as hell do have is the authority to order this water. I snag Dwayne's gun off the floor, it connects, and I try scanning under his user number. Same exact thing.

1974 San Francisco

The Flyers took the Bruins in game six for the '74 cup. That was weeks ago, and hockey gave full-way to baseball season. Joe doesn't care enough to listen on the radio.

The air is warming as much as San Francisco spring will allow. With the windows rolled all the way down in the Datsun, parked on top of Russian Hill, Joe thinks about what Vicky said to him that night they went to get a drink... about if they were right to come out here from Boston and if they were wrong to stay.

Something always drew him to the gigs guaranteed not to pay off—not that he had much to show for the ones that did. By now, he could spot the destined to fail cases: starting off with the largest promise of financial gain, the easiest of times, most convenient of circumstances—all bust to hell after the appearance of a distant third cousin or illegitimate step-daughter come home. No invoices to send. Lucky if he even held onto the retainer by the time Boston's Finest had a go at him.

This one had been different. Not only because of the stickler lawyer—with his buttoned cuffs and bifocals and the kind of dark hair that stays put even after removing a hat several times in a day—who offered no big promises and guaranteed only that his employer's checks would be valid for 90 days, including the one for retainer already written out for 25 grand.

They didn't hesitate. He can remember that. Decisions are made in an instant, whether well thought out or unforeseen.

Joe had, "decided the instant I saw the check."

"You were decided before the guy ever knocked on the door," Vicky told him.

She was right. It's not like they weren't waiting for him... for anything. The '50s must have been a good time to have a kid. Why not join in? If they knew what the '60s had in store, they might have thought twice. Even before involvement in Vietnam, life in the US was pretty turbulent. Most of the gigs they took back then were missing persons, dicey to begin with, and always the potential of turning homicide. As the war effort intensified, the hearts and minds in Boston became more concerned with staging minor revolutions on Storrow Drive or occupying the Northastern Campus. Missing persons were mostly those dodging draft notices, not really the stuff where a private investigator gets involved. General misconduct dropped fairly low on the radar of the Finest and filled the office with speed freaks looking for stolen cash from bad deals, parents looking for their tweaker kids—which usually meant OD, guys who were shot that needed a doctor referral, producing not what you would call an atmosphere conducive to healthy child-rearing.

They sent the kid at less than 10 years old to live with his grandfather Joe in the suburbs of western Mass, deciding it was their best chance at keeping him from inheriting the family business.

Just fine, for a while.

It soon became clear that the income from drug addict clientele and the old man's social security checks wasn't enough to cover the cost of progeny. Vicky took a third job. Joe moonlighted as undercover security at nudie clubs around the Combat Zone. They tried as good as anyone might. But no matter how hot they burned both sides of the candle, it was never enough to make ends meet. The lease was up on the downtown office by the time Martin Abraham, Esq. found them, brushing past the custodian scraping the *E* in Burke off the glass of the office door with a putty knife.

Abraham's contracts were signed. His check was cashed. A trust was set up for the kid, most of the rest went to Joe Sr. for raising the boy. Joe and Vicky made it to the West Coast on fumes, and Mr. Abraham took care of them from there.

"More money will come. It'll be wired under a phony name. I can't tell yet how often, but it'll come," Joe told his old man.

"What about his parents? How often he's gonna see them," Joe Sr. asked him.

"The kid can have parents or starve. What would you choose?"

"Both. Parents and not starve. That's what your mother and me did for you."

"Times were different then."

"Not that different."

"Things change."

"But you don't."

They grew accustomed to living slightly in the costly city on the expenses provided by Abraham. They received regular payments and netted a respectful nest egg for the boy. Enough to see him through teen years, college—and if he wanted to—grad school.

Three thousand miles away: two mountain ranges, a few times zones, an entire continent. The kid was a man now, could take care of himself. Wouldn't he want to know his family? But Joe had the experience to prove, the powers that be have a much more far-reaching hand than the most extraordinary person. If Nestlé came knocking, the best thing for the kid would be ignorance and not feigned. Though they never said it out loud, both Vicky and Joe knew the best way they could provide for their family was to not be their family at all. Keep the checks coming, keep the future open, try to make a change so that the kid would stand a chance if he had a family of his own someday. Family life, comfort, safety—if there was such a thing. Not a legacy, but a couple of generations at least of their blood passing through the veins of time. So, they stayed. Hadn't paid the toll to use the bridge in years. No Ghirardelli at the wharf. No day trips to Alcatraz. Established no connections, kept no subscriptions. Left the rented apartment to eat and to work.

It wasn't until the end of last year that Abraham hit them with the news that his employer would expect Vicky to testify in court. A lawsuit being arranged by—Joe suspected on nothing more than a hunch and Abraham's accent—a U.K. media outlet's private interests. *The War on Want* hit piece helped solidify his belief in his own ideas.

He had waded deeper shit than this for nothing. Now things were paying off, and he felt that he had nothing to show for it. Whatever held him back held her too. She could have said day one or today to give it up, and he'd have gave.

Yet, the clack of her ascending pumps in his ear.

Every family the same, he thought. She said, each one worse

23

than the last. It could have been that none were different than the other, only the sameness of them not being her family—her son—was weighing on her more each time.

The familiar cheap wood knock of the apartment door.

She would say:

"Hello. I'm Victoria, your loving Mother Craft nurse."

But she doesn't.

Zipping fabric noise as the concealed microphone is yanked out from beneath the pressed white smock. Radio static. Joe hurdles himself from the car. The tape recorder hits the pavement, tape skitters out. The door to the Datsun is wrenched from the hinges. The initial thwack of a side-view mirror he feels, but not much else after that. Like local anesthesia. You're going to experience some slight discomfort. Joe discomforts himself along half the length of a Chevy delivery van before succumbing to physics several feet away. His body slumps over once on the steep incline but doesn't roll. Earpiece still in his ear, wire trailing off to nowhere...

1988 Boston, MA

The soft-focus vignette wore off long ago.
Perpetual, blunt inebriation.

"...that's the difference, I tell you the truth. To exist down here is one thing, but you gotta remember stuff is white and black. And that man called me a racist. Me! I told him it's good and evil. That's all it is. God is great and will do good, and Satan is evil and will do such, and when I flipped my F-150 to avoid running over that little colored girl on the scooter, I knew God was between me and that asphalt in the form of one-half inch, American made and manufactured steel."

"A lot of that steel comes from Germany," the Old Man at the next stool from the spewing racist has quietly taken all he could.

The slack jaw waggles in misunderstanding, "What's that?"

"The Ukraine too," the Old Man informs him.

"The U... crane?"

"Soviets. You should try praying to Lenin instead."

That's too much for this guy, who puts an end to the discussion by standing up so abruptly he spills the better part of both their beers across the dated mahogany. He lays down some cash without tip, "God hates Pinko fucks."

The Bartender enters from somewhere beyond the fish-eyed semi-clarity of a years long drunk to wipe up the booze. Gets a clean glass and fills it, "Refill on the house."

The voice doesn't belong this close to the Prudential Tower. More like Dorchester. 15 minute train ride. Upper-class salvation glimpsed in nightly tips from the almost white-collar, financial district, dive bar scene.

"Why don't you make it the last for tonight, Old Man."

"Huh-uh..." the Old Man grunts.

"Pay up after that."

Old man. An acceptable assessment. He's been old-ing up the place every night this week. A place he knows from when he was a kid. He wasn't supposed to come to Boston, but who would recognize him now? Old man.

He found the man he wanted easily enough: James Winston, financial advisor for multiple firms throughout the Seacoast and Tri-State areas after stepping down from his former position as CFO of Nestlé NA Northwestern division more than a decade ago.

People establish natural routines. Tax maps, parking tickets, offense history all publicly available if you know where to look. Enough to build a foundation. City and state, zip, street, job, route, grocery, barber, bar.

James Winston walked in less than a half-hour ago. Sat down and took a booth past the end of the bar to read a newspaper.

Winston doesn't look up from a wrinkled copy of *The Herald* when the Old Man approaches and hovers over his table.

"I don't have any money," the paper ruffles.

"How 'bout a drink?"

"Why don't you get a job?"

"My treat, Jimmy. We'll have that drink," the Old Man motions to the Bartender across the room. "A couple of beers for me and my friend Jimmy!"

"I told you the one you're holding is your last," the Bartender, resolute.

The Old Man glances forgetfully at the mug clenched in his arthritic hand, "One for Jimmy then! Jimmy can have one."

The Bartender crosses ropey working arms across his chest.

The Old Man rolls his eyes and turns to his new friend, "Don't worry, Jimmy, we'll sort this out." He approaches the bar. "What'd we owe you to get another? What'd I have today? Four?"

"That's the tenth in your paw there now."

"Okay... alright, plus one more for Jimmy. What do you want, James Winston? One of those micro-shit drafts they got?"

Winston doesn't respond. He casts a defensive eye across the few looks he's earned being hollered at by the old drunk.

"Nah, Jimmy's a local boy. Give him a Sam Adams in a bottle. Here's $40 bucks. That should cover us."

The Bartender stuffs the hefty tip in his front pocket. He pops the lid off two bottles of Boston Lager and slides them over the bar. The old man gulps what's left in the mug and leaves it to be cleaned. Winston puts the paper down and accepts the bottle when the Old Man returns.

"Anything good today?"

The Old Man tugs the paper out from under Winston's arm.

James Winston has had enough. "I don't know what you think this is, Gould. Going around like some self-righteous process server handing out unsubstantiated blackmail threats like divorce papers. However you think this whole thing looks from the outside... it doesn't... and it's not working."

Gould levels swimming eyes at Winston over the editorial section. It occurred to him that Winston didn't seem as shocked as the others to see him. Considered that his actions were beginning to cause preceding murmurs beyond his most recent confrontations.

The scuttlebutt in Ohio was laced with his nom du jour. He almost called the whole thing off in Indy when a stranger on Washington Street asked if he knew where to get a good drink of water. When he landed at Logan and rented a car, he was followed through the Callahan back into town.

"Just fine."

The name Kirk Gould still drew some attention from the long active members of the major publications in any city, but Boston was his home, and it didn't take more than nothing at all to pull a couple hard-earned favors from his former associates—but let's not call them friends—who were willing to have that debt ticked off their scroll.

Winston picks at the label of his beer with his thumbnail.

Slouched, eyes on the backs of his hands.

"You think anyone cares about some smear campaign from the '70s? Why don't you go back to Cupertino or wherever you're from and quit pretending you're a journalist. You barely were when they would print you."

Gould folds the paper over in fourths with a crease, finds his smokes and chooses a Marlboro from the array of brand names bummed here and there throughout the day. He lights up with a match. A little stale, but good. It doesn't take Winston as long to find what he's looking for: bottom right quadrant of the front page. No continuation. No page-break. A caption that does most of the work for a photo distorted for censure. The article isn't overdone but draws the eye:

Trusted Boston CFO wanted for embezzlement of corporate funds to finance sex trafficking organization...

Photo Credit–Source
Writing Credit–Kirk Gould

The accompanying image is a layout of three thumbnails. The first is that of one, James Winston—a corporate business card mugshot—staring right back at himself. The two smaller images depict Winston with what appear to be underage women in unwholesome circumstances, their faces heavily distorted for privacy. There isn't much more to the article. The case is developing, and any information about Winston's whereabouts is asked to please be reported to the authorities.

"You want a Newport or a Camel," Gould asks, poking at the labeled bands of the cigs.

"This isn't true. Isn't real."

Gould leans across to get a better view of the column.

"Says it right there, Jimmy. Must be real."

"You think anyone will believe that I..."

"That's not you in the picture right there? Looks like you."

Gould takes the paper and holds it up next to Winston's face.

Winston bats the paper away, "This isn't how extortion works, you God damned psychopath. As though there was anything I could tell you to begin with. This is slander."

"It sure is. Pretty well done, I might add. Not the least compelling crock of shit ever editorialized."

"And you think this will stick?"

"No. But it'll be real slimy 'til it washes away."

"You didn't want to ask anything? About..."

"The Arrowhead land deed? You couldn't tell me anything I don't already know. Like you said."

"That's it then? The article and nothing? No choice?"

"Do I have to extend an anecdote?" Gould taps the Newport— his least favorite—out of the pack and lights it up for Winston, "Being a fall guy is probably the best thing you ever did. And you're doing a damn fine job at it."

"I should be angry, I guess."

"Are you angry?"

"Shocked. If I'm angry, I can't feel it yet."

"Some guys might cry."

"I won't do that."

"Or pull a piece..."

"I bet a lot would do that."

"Some."

"I won't. I don't even have one."

"It's probably for the best. I don't think the guy behind the bar would let you get the thing out of your sock."

Winston drinks his beer and smokes his Newport. He uses the restroom, and leaves.

Gould hangs around in the booth for a while. He knows about the San Bernardino deed. Nestlé acquired the right to pump some millions of gallons annually from Lake Arrowhead back around 1900 and paid some joke price of about $500 bucks a year to do it. The permit's up for renewal, and as several past interviews have revealed, the company is not looking forward to any price negotiations and even less to the updated environmental impact study, which would surely be required.

Gould finishes his beer. Thinks about asking for another but decides against it in favor of leaving on the highest note possible. Winston isn't waiting out on the street or around the corner. Gould shambles cautiously the few blocks to the Common. Most of the park visiting types have migrated home for the evening, leaving a few scattered homeless sprawled out in various, warm late-day sun napping positions.

Had he expected it to be like this? Yes.

He knew when he started, eventually threats wouldn't be enough.

If getting started is the first step to getting ahead, then why did everything he started always bite him in the ass?

Experience teaches a lesson that may never be learned.

As he looked back on the course that helped form the person he was today, it wasn't only unclear what the lesson had been but, more importantly, the result.

A better student would have avoided The Common, would be stepping off the Greyhound at Logan: Domestic Departures. Never would have come to Boston to begin with. But Gould was a failure at doing the right thing.

It didn't take long for them to appear.

Materializing from the shadows of duck boats and maple trees.

Agents of the enemy. Tough Guys sent to do tough stuff.

If he can make it to the Park Street Church, Gould thinks, he could lose them in the cemetery beyond. He crosses the Freedom Trail's last stretch on this side of the park, barely avoiding a herd of spandexed bicyclists. A few yards of grass before asphalt sanctuary. The last of the transplanted elms.

He's caught before reaching the sidewalk.

The three closest to him move in. Freshly shaven razor burn. White collars. Black tie. Black gloves. Cut... just like a knife. The steel is sly and intrusive. Canvas, cotton, skin, flesh: opened for the unwelcome guest. The drunk is deep, but the blade is deeper.

"This is a warning you don't deserve, Gould," the Toughest Guy says when the handle goes as far as it can.

"You're supposed to rough a guy up first," Gould opines, "I was recently having a similar conversation regarding extortion."

The blade comes out, and the handle comes down on his cheek. The Toughest Guy lets him fall to the ground. It hurts to breathe, but he does. Can't taste blood, but enough is draining from the slit in his lower abdomen to be worried about.

"Whatever limp-dicked story you're trying to bullshit ain't gonna happen. Got it, fuck-o? No baby killer shit, no bottling plant shit, no land deed shit. You think anyone outside of San Bernardino even knows where it is? Buncha' friggin' redneck bad motor scooter riding hicks out there don't even care, why should you? Stay out of Boston. Stay out of Indiana. Stay out–"

"Stay out... stay out, I get it," Gould interrupts. "Christ. If you're not gonna kill me, leave me alone already."

The Tough Guys silently confer. The Toughest passes off the knife to another before the group begins to re-blend into their respective surroundings. Gould presses hard on his belly and stands. He shrugs the overcoat off his shoulders and ties it around his waist. Blood soaks through the heavy canvas.

"Yeah, jobs over," he calls after them. "Good work. Checks come out Thursday. Where does Abraham find you clowns?"

The Toughest Guy stops, considers the insinuation. He wants to say something cute, Gould can tell. Wants to get the last word and what he's got is probably a good one. He doesn't. Keeps his mouth shut. Resumes his no-place in the crowd.

Gould makes it as far as the street before having to hunch over on a parked car for support. He looks both ways for traffic before crossing Park Street, thinking, if he passes out in front of the church, at least they'll say a prayer, or better yet, get him some medical attention.

2015 Saugus, MA

Wild Oats makes a good eggplant-Parm, which hits the spot at 7:30AM. I browse the bulk nuts and pick up a few dates, some almonds. They carry all the hippy-dippy shit you don't find at my store: flax, matcha, turmeric. I get a box of ginger tea and some fair-trade Colombian whole bean. While passing the free-range eggs, which I never buy because of the price—sorry chickens—I can't resist the urge to remove a displaced 12pack of bottled water half leaning into the dairy cooler. Store brand water, end of the aisle display two aisles over. A habitual glance takes note of the UPC. Ingredients: (naturally sourced spring water), Minerals (added for taste). Distributed by: Wild Oats Markets.

I finished the eggplant before ever getting off Main Street, driving with my knees wedged under the wheel of my old Ford Explorer most of the way. The low mist that hangs over grass sucked up in the slipstream, commingling with the streaking beads on the fading white acrylic not yet burned off by the sun already high past the horizon of the nearby Atlantic, blown by the wind and exhaust, follows me home. Lights from inside the windows on the first and third floors of the three-story colonial shine in the negative west-facing space not yet invaded by the day. The neighbor below me, who I never saw, had some regular-ish day job that he apparently drove back and forth to every day. Left after I went to sleep, went to sleep before I left. I pass his door on the way up unfinished pine steps tacked on when the home was converted to a complex.

I put the Wild Oats bags in the kitchen, throw the cold stuff in the fridge, and fill an electric kettle from a filter attached to the tap. I take off my bra and tug it out my shirtsleeve, tossing it, catching a loop on the back of a wooden chair near the front door. The speaker of my Macbook trumpets as it powers on. While the tea steeps, I open Safari and Wikipedia:

Wild Oats Markets, Inc.

The results are plain.

Wild Oats was a natural foods store from Colorado back in the '80s before expanding into other states through the '90s. They promote a healthy lifestyle and ethically sourced coffee and all that crap we buy into from websites. The soda distributors were the major ones associated with brands like Coke, Dr. Pepper, Sprite—distribution being affected regionally because those soda companies use different distributors across the country.

According to several articles listed in the top results from Google, the Wild Oats past was pretty spotless, free of controversy. They were caught up in some minor FTC intervention when a committee found that a purchase of the company by Whole Foods would violate antitrust laws, and Whole Foods was forced to re-sell, passing it off to Wild Oats' largest shareholder, the owner of a venture capital firm well versed in the field of grocery-chain mergers. They did have a significant shift in manufacturing when they expanded east, but that was centered around Golden Pastures, a Noblesville Indiana dairy farm. Wikipedia lists Wild Oats in their client roster along with some of the bigger stores like Kroger, Pavilions... Stop & Shop.

Keys rattle outside, scratch at the knob, missing the keyhole. The key finds the slot, and the door swings open, banging into a well-established dent in the drywall.

"Burke, your internet working? Mine's shit the bed, girl."

Maritza was my landlord, my neighbor on the third floor, a tweaker, and no matter how often I changed my locks, always had keys to my apartment. Her teeth were surprisingly intact for a regular meth user of her age, which I guessed was over 50 but in all honesty could have been 40 'cause like, of fucking meth.

"I don't have internet, you know that."

"How you on Wikipedia then, bitch?" Her mouth works over her gums.

"I use a hot-spot," I hold up my iPhone.

"Can you watch Netflix on it?"

"Not really. It takes up a lot of data-"

"That's like, streaming and shit? So why you think mine's out then?"

"Did you make sure the modem's plugged in?"

"Yeah."

She hadn't.

"Did you unplug it and plug it back in?"

"Yes, I unplugged it and plugged it back in. Damn, girl! Would you help me please?"

"If it's more than that, I can't help. Did you pay the bill?"

She mouthed something neither of us could hear, lids batting away the shutter vision.

"Actually, that's what I came down here for... you know the rent is due."

"Rent isn't fuckin' due, Maritza. I paid you two days ago."

I pull up the photos on my iPhone and swipe past the last 10 or so images until I land on one of me and Maritza in an awkward selfie standing outside on the back stairs. We look at the camera, smiling. An unsealed envelope passes between us, several hundred dollar bills fanning out the top. The front of the envelope clearly marked in black sharpie: *Burke–Rent–March*

Maritza stares down at the screen. Scratches absentmindedly at a spot on her jaw, "What you doin' tonight?"

"Working, same as every night."

"Bitch, you need to get yourself a man," her attention now on the bra dangling from the back of the nearby chair.

"Work in the nighttime, sleep in the daytime. Ain't got time for that now."

She reaches out and touches the fabric band of the bra. Held it between her thumb and finger. Fucking touched my underwear.

"It's not like you're seeing anyone," she became like, partially conscious of what she was doing. Put her hands in her pockets. "Men are good for thirty seconds when they're hard, and that's about it. A fuck on Saturday and a limp dick all week. And like God, they rest on Sunday, so who the fuck needs 'em?"

"I guess that's what it is then," I agree.

"Girl, come look at my modem or whatever. Fix this shit, please. The *Real Time with Bill Maher* show is on from last night, and I want to watch it before I go to work."

"You don't work!"

"Well, I still want to watch it, girl damn!"

"Alright. I'll come plug your modem in again. After that, I'm going to bed, so stay the hell outta here."

I walk past her, snagging the keys from where she left them in the doorknob, slide mine off the ring, toss the rest to her. She jangles the keys around, trying to get them in a pocket, and follows me outside.

I close the door and lock it, "You like that *Real Time* show?"

"Yes, bitch... you gotta stay informed."

The laptop disconnects from the hot-spot as I climb the steps, drawing the signal away. A dialogue box on the screen reports the lost connection and suggests scanning for available networks. The web pages in the background display 404 errors. After a minute, battery saver settings begin to dim the screen, which soon fades to black.

*

A week had gone by since I thought of where the water came from. Pallets kept rolling off the truck, the balance kept getting adjusted—another thing I didn't have to worry about. I meant to bring it up to management, but what good would that do? The computer does most of the ordering anyway, as good an excuse as any...

It was my night off, and I was expecting a package: the new Criterion Blu-Ray release of *Dr. Strangelove or: How I Learned to Stop Worrying and Love the Bomb, 1964–Stanley Kubrick*, so it was a bummer when the brown paper shipper revealed a 23andme home testing kit since I had already watched both *Ace in the Hole, 1951–Billy Wilder* and *Breathless, 1960–Jean-Luc Goddard*, but also pretty weird because I hadn't ordered a 23andme home testing kit despite my name on the shipping label, invoice, and a welcome kit that like, folded out of the clinical cardboard box. A call to 23andme customer service confirmed that the kit had been intended for me and was, in fact, one of many purchased by a person whose profile I could review after I registered and submitted my sample to the DNA database.

"Likely someone trying to establish their family tree," the Customer Service Rep told me.

But that's all they were allowed to say, and more information would be available online once I registered and if others who received the kits like, participated. There was a registration code on the shipping box directing me to a lengthy sign-up process during which I agreed to release varying degrees of rights to my precious bodily fluids if I did indeed decide to spit into the provided collection vial.

Name: Jo Burke
Sex: Female
DOB: 11/28/1984
Hair: Black
Eyes: Blue
Place of Birth: Massachusetts

The rest of the categories were all non-applicable, in that, they truly didn't apply. I mean, they probably did. I'm sure there are or were at some time a man and a woman out there who knew each other long enough to at least fuck once. I just didn't know who they were. My old man... my adoptive father, finally showed me my original birth certificate not too long before he died. I guess he wanted to have everything out in the open. His name was Joe, too.

Ma didn't stick around long after that, and in keeping with her tight-lipped upbringing, didn't provide any insight into the past. As far as she saw it, she was my mother, always had been, and a birth certificate wouldn't change her mind about it.

That doesn't mean at times I wasn't still curious about like, where I came from. The government institution type birth certificate I was provided with was for a woman named Jane Smith at the State Hospital out in Worcester. Committed anonymously by an anonymous party. At least that's the information the state made available for public record.

"Should I go out there? Is she still there," I asked my old man.

"What's the difference if she is?"

"I could meet her. Learn about who I'm gonna be."

"Everything about who you're gonna be, you got from your mother and me."

The NPR broadcast on the kitchen radio conceals the sounds of my mother discreetly listening from beyond the adjoining door.

"What about like, genetics? That place is a fuckin' nuthouse, right? Who knows what kind of whackos they have locked in there."

"Easy with that. It's where we got you..."

"I feel like there's more I could know."

"Anything you need to know comes to you in time."

"Or I could go find out for myself."

"Have we ever stopped you?"

Nah. They hadn't. And I didn't follow up.

I did wonder sometimes. Called over to Worcester State a couple times, never making it further than the pre-recorded touch-tone menu. Took the hour-long bus ride out to the newly renovated grounds, imagined the place when it was still ominous and Gothic. My first home.

I wanted to stop the orderlies on their mid-shift breaks and ask how long they'd worked there. How far back did the records go? Were any of the patients transferred to the new facility after the renovation? Did I remind them of anyone?

But I wouldn't ask. Never even set foot inside the remodeled hospital. Just stood staring up at the historic clock tower, preserved from the original admissions building, letting the Marlboro butts pile up until it was time to catch the Greyhound back to Boston. Took my old man's advice and let the history of my would-be mother go on undisturbed.

1990 Boston, MA

This area was supposed to be improving.

The residual effects of redlining and class discrimination were running their course unchecked. Gentrified Cambridge seems like a thing of the very distant future. Corners of polyethylene snap in the wind off the harbor. Pools of stale rainwater bubble under the aged roofing skin. Joe Burke Jr. has been laid out on his stomach scuffing the toes of his Clarks for the better part of an hour. At 18 floors, with the telephoto lens zoomed in through a drainage culvert in the low coping, he can see over the Charles past Storrow drive, into Beacon Hill: boaters gathered at the public dock up the river from the Hatch Shell. Pre-requisite sailboats, rowing crews, launched and returned.

Choppy water spray fills the viewfinder with crystal distortion until the clouds move over, bringing Gulf weather from the south. A rare but welcome change from the brisk season to all but the boaters who have to lower their sails, retreating to the docks and the snack bar, holding out hope for clearer skies, though the looming thunderhead is already sparking electric.

All those yachting caps and windswept locks milling around confuse the frame, making it difficult for Burke to find focus.

"Just fine," he thinks, panning the crowd.

His targets make themselves easy to spot, choosing not to assimilate to the general aesthetic. Town-car'd over from the financial district, the capital building. Two suits, stiff and formal, shoulder padding their way through the irresolute river crowd.

The camera starts snapping as the men near each other, follows glad-hands into breast pockets. Parcels exchanged. No words spoken. He recognizes the slickest of the two as a state senator.

The other, an industrialist?

Regulatory committee goon?

Anti-union influencer?

He couldn't be sure... wasn't his job to be sure. Journalism established whatever facts were necessary and paid Burke half up-front for his services. Photo documentation of the clandestine exchange was all the supporting evidence needed to sway public opinion.

Joe hadn't found much use for opinion in his career. Tail the mark to the wrong side of town, the husband to the wrong bedroom, mayor to the wrong card game. He usually stayed detached. No use judging anyone's principles; he'd have to spend some time judging his own first.

The career of private investigator held much more mysticism when his license was first issued. The movers hauling the chestnut executive desk up to the third-floor office of a Beach Street walk-up. The custodian painting *BURKE* on the glass of the door. The smell of sweet cake from the Chinese bakery downstairs was new and enticing. Pork belly steamed buns for lunch every day would never get old, and the tobacco the old men on the stoop rolled in a brand of papers Joe didn't recognize beat the hell out of his stale Marlboros.

He struggled to recall the experience and how it felt at the time. Before the exhaust of the bakery turned sickly. Before the unrelenting tobacco smoke tinged by fried pig permeated his tweed so he smelled like a tannery no matter how many times he patronized the Chinese Laundry downstairs.

He planned to hire a girl to work the desk in the stuffy anteroom. She could have brightened the place up, a plant in the window or a throw rug hanging on the wall like it was a piece of art, or any one of those decorate-y things people do. Strictly business. Not that he wasn't open to an amorous exchange from time to time in what was left of the Combat Zone a few blocks away, but found that raising a daughter required even more time and attention than a girl on the side ever would allow.

The anteroom remained stuffy. The *E* in Burke had begun to peel a long time ago, and the custodian was never able to be found. Prospective clients dedicated enough to navigate the paper lamps and crispy ducks, past the crates of fireworks jumbled up the stairs, let themselves in, didn't bother to shut the door behind them.

The Senator travels without an escort, not noticing the late model Chevelle a few cars back. Joe gooses the SS396 through a couple of red lights to keep up with the immaculate Benz as he follows the Senator on his daily errands. A couple of stops around the financial district, gas station, Bank of America. Joe finds a spot across the street when the Benz parks outside a nondescript office building: campaign headquarters for the upcoming down-ballot election, which will earn the Senator a second term so long as the winds of influence blow his financial resources in the right direction. The politician locks the Benz, tests the handle to ensure, and heads inside without paying the meter.

Joe doesn't waste any time, jaywalking across Boylston, posting up in a shuttered doorway, sparking up a Marlboro, casually observing the city life passing him by. He waits until the Senator is out of sight before approaching, kneels near the rear fender, feigning an untied lace on one of the Clarks. A hand under the chrome bumper finds an electrical wire running up into the frame. Joe yanks the wire loose; rises to inspect the interior of the Benz through the back window.

A collection of paperwork and cheeseburger wrappers litter the upholstery and floor mats: campaign buttons, bumper stickers, election mailers. A worn leather briefcase leans on the console between the front seats.

The slim-jim fits snugly up his sleeve, bending at the elbow. He slides it out his cuff and straightens the flat metal, gently inserting the hooked tip between the window and the rubber seal, careful not to leave a scratch on the painfully maintained chrome window trim. The lock pops after some brief finagling. The alarm system does not sound off.

Joe sits in the passenger seat with the door open, briefcase on his lap. He's able to bypass the three-wheel lock they slap on these things to give the purchaser a sense that their Ritz crackers and bar graphs will be secure by holding the latch-release and feeling for tension in the combo wheels. After both sides are set to the appropriate ones and zeros, the latches open.

Antacids, cigarettes, pens and paper, scratch-pad, a charge card tucked away in a back slot, a check-book with hastily folded receipts poking out of the folds. Joe lays the receipts out inside the briefcase and takes a couple of photos of the whole collection with his Kodak Ektralite.

"These'll get us front page. Want an advanced print?"

Curtis Donavan slides the negatives back in with the photos. An Emerson-grad looking *Herald* investigative journalist: better haircut than Joe, suit fits better; three-figure yearly salary so long as some fresher, better fitting suit-wearing haircut doesn't come along too soon. He pays in cash and lights a Parliament, joining Joe for a smoke they won't finish.

"Skip it," Joe pockets the cash without looking.

"Not interested in the fruits of your labor?"

"The new wine? Dying on the vine..."

"Whatever with you then."

"My bad, Don man."

"No one said you gotta be a snoop."

"I know it."

"You think I like sitting on my butt all day coming up with synonyms for corruption?"

"Conception," Joe offers.

"Right. Funny."

"You hate it so much, then change. You got a degree."

"Degrees don't get jobs. If I left *The Herald*, I'd be proofing the *Stop & Shop Weekly Circular*." Donavan flicks ash from the cig. The T swooshes past overhead, third rail fizzling after it's gone.

"Ever consider re-enlisting?"

"And get sucked into another civil war? No thanks. Is that what you're thinking? Signing up again?"

"I haven't been thinking much lately."

"This is news?"

Joe removes a steel flask from his jacket, passes it after taking a hit. Donavan grimaces when he passes it back.

"Good though, right?"

"What the hell is it?" Donavan wipes his mouth.

"Mekappy or something like that."

"Tastes like rotten apples."

"That's what Mr. Lee says."

"Still working out of Chinatown?"

"If you can call it that... it's cheap, low-key."

They drink.

"I hear they're already contracting transport crews out there in Kuwait. Might be for the long haul. You could rack up a good chunk of change in a few years."

"Nah, I can't leave JoJo like that."

"Look, man," Donavan tosses the Parliament before the filter, "I gotta go. But before I jet... I got a tip from a copywriter a few floors up. Something to do with you. Guy's an old-timer... Ace Callahan? Callaway? Something like that?"

"Never heard of him."

"He didn't seem too thrilled to be finding out about you."

"The hell did I do?"

"Beats me... he cornered me today in the parking garage. Guy asks, do I know Burke? I tell him, I know a lot of people. He shoves this at me," Donavan produces a folded sheet of yellow lined paper, "and storms off yelling about for me to tell Burke where to get off and what to do to his mother and all other kinds of old-timer shit-talk."

"Always nice to be thought of. Thanks, Donny."

Donavan starts to walk off, stops, "Whatever it is... if it turns into something..."

"You'll be the first to know."

Neither of them was a worthy candidate for any future wars. Probably neither of them would have ever signed up to begin with if it wasn't for the promise of never actually having to see combat. Willingness to enlist and low-level Boston Metro street crime education was enough to earn speedy rank promotion. The rise of cold war communism after Vietnam all but ensured a role in communications or surveillance for even active-duty Marines; some reconnaissance detail may require their presence in-country on the Russian/Soviet border or Central America.

Would have stayed that way, but they had some buddies killed in the Beirut barracks bombing and were hot under the collar for some misdirected vengeance, volunteering last minute to join the invading forces intervening in the Grenada civil war.

Joe was happy to call it quits with honorable discharge after lackluster service. Donavan found opportunity in field reporting and stuck it out for the potentiality of a transition, which he eventually made. Joe's opportunity came in the form of his first and only daughter. A chance at normalcy, a day job, family life. Cut short in '85 by the death of his wife. Nothing special, a car accident at a failed stoplight. The guy driving the Buick that plowed into her wasn't even drunk. Nobody's fault, really an accident, one of those things that happened. That's what Joe would tell the guy when he'd stop by with flowers or a bottle of Scotch, some candy for JoJo.

The guy never could get over it and ended up killing himself a couple years later. Joe was invited and attended the funeral. Evie would have wanted him to. She would have been there passing out condolences with the reserved compassion that made strangers want to confide in her and loved ones rely on her. All Joe did was smoked a couple of butts, standing in a loose orbit around the grieving family, didn't care to explain how it was he knew the deceased, drinking from a steel flask filled with Scotch the Buick Driver brought him.

He was lucky that his Ma and his old man still had the place out in the 'burbs where they raised him. A place to keep JoJo out of trouble, away from trouble, away from him.

The phone is ringing in the office, questionable considering the increasingly threatening demands from PacBell to pay the overdue bill.

"Been ringing off the hook, all day," Mr. Lee yells from his shop entrance in the lobby. Joe picks up the receiver without greeting. The line sounds clean.

"Joe Burke," a voice on the other end asks.

"You got him."

"You've been approached by Gould?"

"Who is this?"

"You must not come in contact with Kirk Gould, understood?"

"Yeah, sure. Want me to lock myself up at home?"

"It's imperative that you-"

"No problem. I got plenty of canned tuna."

"The safety of your family is at stake..."

"My family? Listen, lady-"

"Gould will contact you. Want to arrange to meet."

"And why can't I?"

"You need another reason?"

"Can I ask what the fuck my family has to do with you?"

"You're the one it has to do the fuck with, smart guy. I'm not getting told, you are. And if it matters to you, then you won't. Their safety. Her safety. Don't go." The line goes dead.

The bills are damp from the heat of his breast pocket. The note is creased, raggedly torn from the notepad. The message, brief. Agitated handwriting speckled with graphite from pressing too hard.

chelsea/terminal
under Tobin
10 p
Kirk Gould

Not one to take advice too willingly, especially from unknown sources, Joe still takes precautions. Gets a taxi to bring him out to Wonderland Station, where he catches The T back into the city, switching trains a few times before heading above ground to hoof the last stretch.

"I won't be around for a few days," he tells Joe Sr. from a payphone. Whoever it was that paid his phone bill, he doesn't trust enough to be using it.

"What's new?"

"Put JoJo on, will you?"

"She's outside with her Grandmother. The O'Neill cat had kittens. They're out there looking at them."

"You gonna tell her I called at least?"

"I'd have to explain who you are first."

"...anyway, I'll be back this weekend."

"We're going to New Hampshire... open up the camp."

"You weren't gonna tell me?"

"I tried asking the operator to ring every payphone in Boston at once, but all I got was librarians and hookers."

"I got a new client. If I wrap it up, I'll meet you up there."

"Why don't you come by next week?"

"Weekdays are tough, you know that."

"We need to sit down, sort some things out."

"What's there to sort out? I'm not talking to Uncle Ben, I told you. I'm no bricklayer."

"You smoking crack out there? After last time?"

"Just fine with me."

"Ben doesn't even run crews anymore."

"I said, just fine."

"We need to talk money, the trust. It's time to sign it over to JoJo. You aren't gonna stop messing around and think of your future? Start thinking about hers."

"I thought you had that handled."

"Everything needs to be in her name now."

"If anything happens, I'll be there for her, you know that."

"I don't know that. I already got it all arranged, when me and your Ma croak, JoJo's going to the Sisters of Divine Grace."

"A convent? I'm not okay with that."

"Good thing I didn't ask."

"I can take care of my own."

"Uh-huh."

"I can, damn it!"

Most pedestrians give a person yelling into the payphone their space. So when Joe becomes aware of some Punk anxiously impinging—rough around the edges enough to ignore social morays without repercussion—he sticks his chin out at him. The Punk taps a finger on the back of his wrist, indicating the time. Joe makes a jerking-off motion with his free hand, indicating to go screw.

" –things we should have got out in the open a long time ago," Joe Sr. is saying. "It's my fault as much as yours."

"No one's done anything wrong."

"I should have listened to your Ma... I'm an old man, Joe. I only got so much time to do things right."

"You're in better shape than me. We got plenty of time."

"No one lives forever, that includes you."

"I'm coming over there. Tomorrow. I'm coming to New Hampshire."

"Okay, kid."

The Punk doesn't wait for the receiver to hit the hook before elbowing past Joe, who, on another day, might have excused it. Would have let the wisecrack slide that he doesn't hear the end of because he's already bounced the Punk's head off the phone terminal. Turns him around, stands him up, and lays him out. Refrains from kicking him in the ribs with the scuffed-up Clarks. Pedestrians flowing past expertly ignore the man in a pile on the ground.

His folks never did care much for his chosen profession. Not to say he was thrilled about it himself. A common path for a guy out of the military, fed up with the rank-and-file corruption seemingly impossible to escape in even the most rural police force, discharged from the same force for not minding playing the game but failing to adhere to the rules. It didn't take much, some forms to fill out, a filing fee, a couple of phone calls to confirm that your references were factual even if you were a loose rock above deplorable. Didn't even have to carry a piece if you didn't want. A healthy relationship at the county clerk's office was more important, a shamelessness about how far you'd follow a lead, the willingness to take a punch every once in a while. Those were the tools of the trade. Could Joe help it if he plied them effectively? It came to him naturally, a couple of favors for old friends, a few requests from strangers through word of mouth.

Joe Sr. kept his opinions to himself, let JoJo stay with them during the weekdays, then weekends, soon it was most nights, and for the better part of the last year, it was all the time. Joe hadn't served enough time for pension, him and Evie didn't have life insurance, never took a dime from the Buick Driver after the accident—had to ask for help from his folks to get her in the ground. He gave Joe Sr. everything he made after rent for a crummy bachelor apartment in Allston and a bottle of Mr. Lee's Ng-Ka-Py. The only substantial thing he had going was a trust his folks set up for him when he was a kid. If he could scrape by long enough without ever having to dip into the reserves, then the trust would be enough for JoJo to get a pretty fair start.

Joe flips his collar up to keep out the chill of the salty air. The intersection of Chelsea and Terminal is a service road crossing beneath the Tobin Bridge on the river's north side. Discreet, with only a small chance of getting stabbed by a needle wielding junkie.

Trash fires burn inconsistently in some of the darkest underpass caverns. Working girls and boys congregate near the dim streetlight corners waiting to get picked up by the freight truckers who've used up their daily driving hours and have to camp for the night regardless of how much No-Doz is still banging in their temples.

The professionals know a cop from a trick, and if they knew Joe wasn't either, he projects enough licensed charisma for the local inhabitants to scatter at his approach. Tremors from the Tobin rumble the asphalt under his feet. He stays in the shadows, concealed in Marlboro smoke. A sedan creeps by, surveying the area for potential bad decisions, speeds away when Joe emerges into the weak incandescence.

It's well past 10p when Gould arrives. Older than Joe by 30 years, disheveled. Dressed like an old-school newspaperman with the faded tails of his beltless trenchcoat flapping behind him. His face, a few days unshaven. Gaunt eyes under a worn felt brim. The creases around his mouth and cheeks exacerbated by daily booze.

Joe draws out the flask for a habitual slug, deftly unbuttoning the clasp on a concealed shoulder holster.

"Never mind the heater, kid," Gould says dismissively, lighting a Marlboro, offering one to Joe from a soft pack, which he accepts. Joe thinks he can see the weight of a piece in the old man's coat pocket but doesn't mention it.

"You're a friend of Callahan's," Joe asks.

"Who?"

"Callaway?"

"Never heard of either."

"There's only one."

"Look, kid. Do you mind if we get this show on the road?"

"It's your thing, man."

Gould smokes thoughtfully.

"You take gigs with *The Herald* a lot?"

"Some."

"Ever do any reporting yourself?"

"Nah."

"How'd you get hooked up there?"

"An old friend. Donavan. Another I thought you'd know."

"You ex-badge?"

"Marines."

"Ever heard of me before?"

"Not before today, and then twice."

"Why twice? You asked around?"

"Didn't have to. After I got your message, I got a call warning me not to show up here."

"A woman?"

"Yeah."

"Amaranth. If she knows, then it's already too late. Come on." Gould begins to walk away, moving fast for an old man with a pretty heavy limp.

"I'm not really supposed to be in Boston, get it?"

Joe tosses the cig and catches up.

"Avoiding this Amaranth lady?"

"Ever heard of the *War on Want*?"

"An equal rights charity or something? Accused of embezzlement a few years ago."

"Jesus Christ, doesn't anybody read..."

"Well, fucking tell me then."

Gould pulls them behind a concrete pillar when a set of headlights come gazing around the corner. He leads them past an overpass-slum to a chain-link fence with a clipped section where he slips through.

"A long time ago, when journalism actually meant something, they were responsible for exposing some big-time corporate shit. Look up the *Want* article on Nestlé and lookup an article from *The San Francisco Chronicle* – '76 called, *Don't Cry Over Spilled Blood*, my name. Find Abraham." Gould stops in a public parking lot out by the docks. "Got a drink?"

Joe gives him the flask.

Gould doesn't flinch at the taste.

"Amaranth's gonna make it a pain in the ass to keep in touch. Look up the articles I told you. Find Abraham. When the time's right, we'll meet again. Not in Boston." He takes another swig and hands the flask back to Joe, "Thanks, kid," he turns to go.

"What about a retainer? Other clients pay half up-front."

"You don't have any other clients..."

Joe lights a smoke, watching him go. Maybe it was best, he thinks, to meander back to Chinatown and take the Chevelle up to New Hampshire tonight. He'll look up the articles on Monday. Whatever story Gould's been trying to cook up for the last decade wasn't going to get resolved this weekend.

His old man was right. He had to think about JoJo's future, his family's future. For that, Gould could wait.

Rattling chain-link breaks Joe from his thoughts. Screeling white-walls rip into the lot, bumper sending sparks from the asphalt. Gould looks back over his shoulder. Joe steps forward, already gripping the .45 under his jacket, but Gould shakes his head, no. The old man plunges his hand into the front pocket where Joe knows he has a Colt Special. The short cut barrel repels the Metro night, tracking the driver's window of the blacked-out Charger burning radials in a 180° degree spin. The rubber paints a brief infinity where the tires crisscross.

Gould wrenches the heavy trigger, assigning all five chambers to a single point. The driver's window shatters before the chassis finishes revolving. Gould lets the spent .38 drop to his side. The Hemi surges against the brake under the dead weight of the driver's sole. Submachine gun fire erupts from the remaining windows. Muzzle flash lightning strobes the scene. Gould jerks erratically as the bullets rip through his shoulder, thigh, abdomen.

Joe balances himself against a nearby truck, arms outstretched over the hood, steadying his aim. The .45 booms when he pulls the trigger, quieting the rat-a-tat assault on the old man collapsing to his knees. Two gunmen emerge from the Charger.

Joe has already changed position, moving laterally. He can see Gould through the tilt of a rearview mirror, splayed out on the ground. Distant sirens announce their intention to intervene.

The two gunmen walk from the Charger with about a meter between them. One sprays 9mm shells from the hip. Bullets ricochet off chrome, rupture tires, split windshields.

Joe pivots out from the cover of a rental RV.

The .45 does the work, guiding his will.

The gun fires once, the action settles, casing pings away. The first man clutches his chest. The gun goes off again, and his head snaps back. Joe moves forward, loosing rounds methodically, closing the gap by the time the remaining target is neutralized.

Gould bleeds a lot, taking shallow breaths at irregular intervals.

The Charger shudders and ticks. The sirens are closer, and Joe wonders if they'll make it in time to help, or if they're coming at all.

He doesn't hear the shot until he's already on the ground. Tries not to visualize the fist-sized divot that surely has been punched out of his back below the shoulder blade by the high-velocity rifle hidden somewhere out of view. His right arm doesn't work, but he can wrestle the flask out of his jacket pocket with his left. Spins the cap off with his thumb and forefinger and raises his head enough to take a hit.

The Ng-Ka-Py does taste like rotten apples, but good. He can't hold the flask anymore and lets it thunk away. He thinks that now may be a good time to meander back to Chinatown and take the Chevelle up to New Hampshire. He'd be outside waiting when JoJo got there in the morning. Help his Ma unload what seemed like an excessive haul for a long weekend in the country. After dinner and a couple of beers with his old man, when the night began to cool over the lake, they'd talk about the future.

The flight was empty, which the guy next to me who wouldn't shut the fuck up the whole trip made sure to point out endlessly.

2015 Indianapolis, IN

I chose not to reveal much personal info to him, like that this was the first time I had ever flown before, first time I left Massachusetts in about 10 years. Hell, before now I had never even taken the obligatory paid vacations offered by Stop & Shop, opting for the equivalent paid out in yearly anniversary checks instead.

It took a long-ass time to get any results from 23andme, which, when they showed up, honestly weren't that impressive. Graphs showing how much Irish heritage I had—a lot. Charts depicting Neanderthal migration patterns alleging what percentage of ancient DNA was present in my bloodline. Tendency of my relatives to enjoy the taste of blueberries and some other worthless tidbits. What wasn't listed was the name of the person who sent the test kit out to begin with. Mostly it was a glorified social media platform where people who had even the smallest percent of genetics in common with you could reach out and try to learn more about their long-lost relations, make sure they hadn't married a not-that-removed cousin, discover their true sexual identity, or harvest some quality leads to catfish on the basis of blood being thicker than common sense.

I had no intention of like, reaching out, or even taking part in the family tree data-gathering exercises that were continually being hocked while scrolling. What did catch my eye in the timeline was a death announced by some lady, a purported third aunt on my maternal biological side. They were having a funeral service for her mother—my grandmother?—Rose, in a couple days, and all were invited to attend.

It wasn't the funeral that got me interested... it's not like I knew these people. What got my attention was the Google Maps hyperlink to the ceremony. Noblesville, Indiana. I knew that town somehow but couldn't remember. My browsing history came up with one result from almost a month ago: the Wikipedia entry for Wild Oats Markets. Golden Pastures Farm—Noblesville, Indiana. I could have resisted the confluence... chalked it up to universal persuasion. But when a FedEx package arrived the next day—overnighted with an Indiana PO Box as a return address—containing tickets for a round trip flight from Logan to IND-X, I had to give in to temptation.

The guy from the seat next to me followed me all the way off the plane and through the terminal, continuously yapping about some business he had in Indy and how a revitalized Mass Ave was going to save the city from becoming another memory of community surrounding a stadium. Yuppy-ville for sure if this guy was any representation. I lost him in the food court, veering off to one side of an Indy 500 stock car displayed on a pedestal in the middle of the atrium. Kept an eye on him the whole way down the escalator, making sure he didn't catch up to me after he hit baggage claim.

I picked up a car rental and was entering Noblesville inside an hour. This was the kind of small-town you think of when you think, small town. Norman Rockwell shit all the way, with one commercial street bookended by a church and a town hall; fairly empty for a Friday afternoon. The only place on the whole block with a car in the lot was a diner with a sign over the door that read, *DINER*. I pulled the nondescript Chevy Impala rental up to the curb, avoiding the lot. A Waitress worked the counter through the plate-glass windows that framed either side of the screen door entrance.

I nodded to her.

She either didn't notice or didn't care.

I lit up and smoked on the sidewalk, examining tin Coca-Cola advertisements leaning in the windows. The diner was one of the only buildings on the street that didn't look like it had been converted from a former residence. Across the street, an apparent beautification effort resulting in a couple bougie-ish brunch spots, a hand-made clothing store, specialty greeting card and trinket shop. Entrapments for the well-bred Chicagoan on the way back to Illinois who wanted a taste of Podunk without having to veer too far from the interstate. Points of pride for the local working-class who commuted all week to Indianapolis and had seen what the yuppy guy's revitalized Mass Ave had done for the city.

"You can smoke in here, Hun," the Waitress hollered through the screen door without leaving her post at the counter.

I took her up on the thrill of a Marlboro enjoyed on a vinyl stool—something not allowed in even the most roughneck local Boston bars.

"Cup of coffee," I asked for when I sat.

She brought a mug and an ashtray. There was one other customer in the whole place, a denim shirted townie down at the far end of the counter. He raised his own mug in casual greeting at my inspection.

"Can I get you a menu?"

"You make a Cobb salad?"

"Sure 'nuff."

"No bacon, no chicken, add an extra egg? Please."

"Suit yourself."

She gave a look to the guy at the end of the counter like, in obvious disapproval, but went to the kitchen and returned quickly with a heaping plate of greens, tomatoes, eggs, cheese, avocado, and some unexpected but appropriate kernels.

The veggies were fresh, and I made short work of the hearty meal. The Waitress took the plate away after I cleaned up the last bits, refilled my mug, and tossed a book of matches on the counter. I lit another smoke, paid in cash, and she brought the change.

"Hungry," the Waitress.

"I guess I was."

"Been on the road long?" She cocked her head at the rental.

"Nah. Landed in Indy a couple hours ago."

"From Rhode Island?"

"Close. Massachusetts."

"Getting so I can almost tell them all apart. Visiting family?"

"Not really... extended family... you know how it is."

"I do."

"I was actually gonna ask, could you help me out? I'm looking for the cemetery. But I get shit for service. Maps hasn't worked since outside of town."

Her demeanor changed. I looked a few stools away for guidance, but my fellow patron was studying his coffee intently.

"You said you was visiting family."

"I did... I am. Some more extended than others, get it? It's a funeral."

"A funeral today?"

"Supposed to be. Look, I don't mean to put you out. If you could–"

"Ain't nobody put out. Cemetery's up the road outside of town. Keep going the way you were comin', you'll find it."

"Cool. Thanks."

She took the remainder of the cash from the counter and pulled the ashtray away before I had a chance to do much ashing. I hung around long enough to gulp down the rest of the coffee, trying to navigate the change in vibe, which was like, wicked moody. The Waitress rested her elbows on the counter down at the far end with the townie. Neither of them acknowledged me again. I left.

"Figures with that bastard dead we'd be done with all their garbage," I could hear the Waitress from outside.

Maybe she wanted me to.

The Waitress didn't lead me wrong, and I found the cemetery not that far out of town. Nothing too extravagant, low granite walls and an iron gate cropped up out of a cornfield stretching uninterrupted to the horizon beyond. An inland sea of gold topped greenery rippling for miles in the breeze. Rustling stalk babel. There were no other cars in the gravel lot. I pulled the Impala right up to the gate and got out, closing the door gently in respect to the calm solemnity of all graveyards.

I wove up and down the grid of tombstones and mausoleums. Mostly bare stones with minimal descriptors, not like the ornate Catholic sites I was used to where my folks were buried.

23andme allowed for a certain level of anonymity, and I never thought to reach out for specifics. Assumed this lady had some event planning sense, seeing as she took the time to reach out to her entire bloodline and Christ knows who else. It's not like I was even interested in learning anything about my fuckin' lineage or whatever... if the test kit hadn't shown up in the mail, I'd have been satisfied keeping my genetics to myself... if I hadn't got unsolicited plane tickets overnighted to me, I would have been pleased to never learn whether or not there factually was more than corn in Indiana—which given my present surroundings, there didn't seem to be.

Fuck it. I had all but given up any curiosity about bottled water distribution... resigned myself to being a high functioning but ultimately unimportant cog in the corporate supply chain...

"Just fine," I muttered out loud.

I was getting close to the gate when I heard the clatter of tools being wheelbarrowed around. A groundskeeper emerged from behind a few of the taller stones in the far back corner.

"Yo!" I shouted, but he didn't acknowledge.

I cut diagonally across the lawn, careful not to step on too many final resting places.

"Pardon me, sir!"

He pushed the wheelbarrow through a back gate and out of sight. I got there in time to see a maintenance truck pull away through the field. The plots in this back corner were the least maintained. Dried flowers rotted and stuck to aged stones, cracked or broken, lopsided or toppled over. Moss grew over the oldest markers. The grass burned in patches where no one bothered to water or seed.

The headstone closest to the back gate was new but cheap-looking, pressed flat down into the ground with no ornamentation. The groundskeeper was obviously finishing a burial. The grass recently dug up. The dirt surrounding the headstone inadvertently kicked and spread around from his work. I had to brush the face clean before I could read it.

The cashier at a nameless gas station on the way to the farm didn't know the Wi-Fi password or even where they kept the router to find out what it was. He did know the way to the farm and gave me written directions, including a little map and even compass points for reference. I bought a cup of burnt coffee and a couple packs of peanut-butter sandwich crackers for the road. I munched half a pack of crackers parked under the canopy shade while attempting to Google:

Martin Abraham, Indiana

Which did yield some search results, but the connection timed out whenever I tried to load the suggested links. I followed the clerk's map, pulling up to the Golden Pastures Farms front office not long after noon. I tried to get connected again while I waited, but the guest Wi-Fi sucked worse than my service. The front office was a converted ranch home with a picture window overlooking acres of grassland hemmed in by a windbreak and like, what else, distant corn fields on every side. A handful of cows grazed around a metal barn that stretched across the property toward a couple towering silos and another smaller barn.

I walked through the pole barn with Mr. Bedrick: the Golden Pastures owner and managing farmer. The front office ranch house used to be his home before expanding operations.

"That's my wife Anitra working the front desk you talked to on your way in."

"No shit?"

"Yup," Bedrick hitched up his Wranglers by the belt—leather with a silver buckle in the shape of the broadside of a cow. He stuck his thumbs in the waistband under a well-fed but not obtrusive belly. "Been a family farm since before the depression. Mom and Grandma kept the whole damned thing alive when Dad got shipped out."

"Must have changed a lot since."

"Welp, when Grandpa first come into it, the whole thing was corn and grain, like all the neighbors. For some reason or another, Grandpa had a helluva' time keeping any of that stuff alive... folks said the soil was junk, said the guy who owned the place before didn't rotate his crop right, said Grandpa was a poor excuse for a farmer..." he stopped and rested a hand on the shoulder height backside of one of the hundreds of cows yoked double file in stations alongside the concrete walkway spanning the length of the barn.

The monotonous passage of cow asses. The smell of methane and wet earth. The sound of dozens of mechanical pumps all sucking udders in unison. I was having some pretty deep thoughts about my relationship with dairy and a hard time paying attention as Bedrick got to the point.

"Mind if I smoke?" I interrupted.

We stood at the far side of the pole-barn looking out over Bedrick's back acres. He smoked a short wooden pipe packed with tobacco he kept in a leather pouch. I smoked a butt. The pipe kept bouncing around under his bushy grey mustache as he talked.

"We've done plenty of upkeep. That tractor barn and those grain silos came with the place. Never did get any real crops to grow… but the grass grew thick, and the cows bred easy. By the time I came around, they had one of the highest yielding dairy farms in the state, and by the time me and Anitra got the place incorporated, it was the highest."

"What's up with that building down there?" I pointed with my cig in the direction of a low concrete warehouse built in a cleared area of the field; a couple refrigerated freight containers parked outside.

"Bottling and distribution. Used to be we worked with a big distributor, was sold all over the country mostly. But nowadays, the big chains want to get you groomed for expansion. If you could produce, say, milk, what they do is throw a little capital your way and get you into the cheese game. After that, little more capital, and they got you growing fruit trees. Soon after, you'd be bottling juice."

"Or water."

"Right you are, or water. We bottled water here through most of the last 20 years. Couple of the big retailers got together— they always get together—and they pay permit and usage rights and all other kinds of junk, and before you know it, you got a water hose running into your dairy barn."

"Did you get to choose what kind of expansion they were grooming you for?"

"Not exactly. Way things work is those grocery chains learned that if they can produce a store brand, then they can compete with a brand name right on the same shelf. Instead of building their own facilities, they expand on one that exists. If things had kept going the way they was, before you know it, we'd have been shipping eggs, meat, juice, you name it."

"You don't bottle water anymore, though?"

"It happened sort of quick. A few letters, a couple of lawyers... before we knew it, trucks were showing up to haul the inventory away. Tell you the truth, I didn't like it much anyway... never felt right... we were practically selling tap water in a fancy package."

"Must have been good money in it for you?"

"Not as much as you think. The real money would have come when we produced more products until eventually we'd get bought out... I didn't like that idea much either. The dairy business saved this farm. It's what I know, got me and Anitra set up pretty nice, got our kids raised and schooled. Someday, if they want, they can take over and do the same for their kids, like my folks done for me."

Bedrick and Anitra walked me out to the Impala after loading me up with some Golden Pastures swag. Bedrick closed the door for me once I was settled inside. I lowered the window to say goodbye.

"Take care," Bedrick leaned on the door frame. "You never did say what paper you're with."

"Paper?"

"Where we can see the story you're doing? I like reading a little dirt... 'specially if I'm involved."

"I don't write for any paper-"

"We was expecting someone to come around, seeing as the funeral was today. Started to wonder what took you so long."

"You knew Abraham?"

Bedrick laughed. He smiled back over his shoulder at Anitra.

"You're a straight shooter, Ms. Burke. Pays to be direct sometimes, don't it? But you know I can't say word one about any of that."

"You could like, point me in the direction of someone who could. I'd keep your name out of it or whatever."

"She's a reporter, no doubt about it. I'd like to be able to say I knew what you was talking about."

"Right. Alright, well, thanks again–"

"Not so fast... the name of the paper?"

"It's uh, a weekly paper, the *S&S Weekly Circular*."

"Must be a back-east thing."

"I'll have to send you a copy."

"You're a long way from home, aren't you, darling," Anitra broke in.

"Speaking of... there a motel around here?"

"Unh-uh, you go on back to Indy. Get yourself a nice comfy room in one of those downtown hotels."

"Beats the Red Roof if you can afford it," her husband agreed.

"I guess I can treat myself."

"You always can," Anitra concluded.

Signs for Indy/Purdue University led the way into Downtown. After getting a room at the Sheraton—the first hotel I found in a circle of them across from the capitol—I took a walk up Mass Ave: mostly brunch spots already closed for the day. College kids packed the few bars that were open to capacity. I wasn't in the mood to be jostled and groped by the polo & shorts crowd and wasn't thrilled by any of the places with kitchens still cooking and soon found myself back at the hotel bar. I ordered a veggie burger and a side of fries with a beer. I got another beer while I finished my fries.

I took advantage of the hotel Wi-Fi and searched:
Martin Abraham, Indiana, Golden Pastures
Results for a bunch of Facebook profiles. Some reverse-lookup ads, ads for ancestry and DNA stuff, Martin Abraham on 23andme. I tapped the 23andme hyperlink and signed-in on a new tab, which redirected me to my account instead of Martin Abraham, and when I searched for him here, the name didn't get any results.

I went and scrolled the DNA relatives wall, but the funeral announcement had been removed. I couldn't remember the name of the lady who posted it, and there weren't even any updates to the wall since two days ago.

Back on Google, I refined the search filters:
News. Last 24 hours. Must include: obituary
The Indianapolis Star returned a bunch of obit' results: mostly old folks who died in their sleep, led rich and prosperous lives, loved by family and friends, active in the community, Elks Lodge, Church potlucks. The kind of 300-word biography we all aspire to peacefully resolve in a future so far removed we smile at the thought of a life well lived being a satisfactory explanation for the more pressing and not often addressed inquiry of like, why at all?
The last article was about a mother and her young son who asphyxiated and died running the heat in their car to stay warm after getting snowed in. Below the article was a little caption:
The previous article is a reprint from our January issue.

Please note an updated time and date for the Henrietta and Jason Butte funeral service. The county coroner's office issued a statement: Due to high intake levels through the winter, deceased persons held for burial until the ground thaw may experience additional processing delays. Please adjust Funeral Services accordingly. Contact your county Coroner's Office for further details.

The Indy Star online archives had issues dating back to the late '90s and downloadable scans dating later than that. I tapped back a few months, starting with January and heading into 2014. Lots of snow-mobile and ice-fishing accidents, pneumonia, car accidents, but no mention of Abraham. So far, my impression of the guy was—known and not cared for. In Noblesville, they got their shit in a twist over the mere mention of the funeral. The Bedricks were weirdly easygoing about the whole thing. You think they'd at least pretend to be bummed about the death of an associate or acquaintance or whatever of theirs. The Indianapolis Coroner's Office didn't have any record of Abraham on file. I tried calling the Noblesville/Hamilton County Coroner, but it was past closing time.

I Googled in a new tab:
background check
Clicked the first link in the list, backgroundcheck.com or something, and paid the $25 dollars to create an account. This time I got a result: Martin Abraham, with an Indiana death certificate. He passed away in the winter up in Noblesville. Cause of death: Natural. There wasn't much else info offered—no aliases or relatives, not even a current address. The last known residence listed was

from like, over 40 years ago: San Francisco, California. Probably not much help.

I Googled around for variations of:
Abraham, Martin, San Francisco, Obituary, Deceased, Death, Passed, Golden Pastures, Water
There were about 20 news sources to sort through, which at first glance didn't have anything to do with the dead man.
The San Francisco Chronicle quickly emerged as the longest-running local paper.

I changed my search terms to:
Abraham, Martin, San Francisco, Chronicle
A lot of stories with partial results popped up but no direct hits.

I put the phone face-down on the bar and had a few gulps of beer, *Goose Island IPA* in a bottle, which I settled for over the lack of my favorite brewery—Harpoon—on the menu. Goose Island had some pretty good offerings, especially in the field of US micro-breweries, which I thought always leaned a little too heavy on the hops. They got their start not far from Indy, one state over in Chicago. I pieced back together the label I had absentmindedly scratched away: Goose Island—Chicago, IL. I spun the bottle, read the blurb on the back about the company's '88 Midwest beginnings—all very tight-knit, beer-lover kind of stuff. The rest of the label was product info. Calories, bottle redemption, ABV, and the last of the small print: Brewed and Bottled by AB InBev. Google revealed AB InBev to be the abbreviation for Anheuser-Busch after an international merger with another company, InBev, in 2008. Since merging, it turns out the subsidiary had been busy acquiring various brands with growing reputations, including Goose Island... fuckin'A.

I popped open a new tab:
profitable, water, subsidiaries, America

Forbes provided some lists for the last few years, with Coca-Cola and Pepsi topping the charts. Exhaustive searches of previous terms, including each company's bottled water aliases—Dasani and Aquafina—came up short. As the ratings progressed, the companies became more varied and regionalized: Poland Springs—New England, Arrowhead—West Coast, Deer Park—Midwest & Southeast, Perrier/San Pellegrino/Acqua Panna—International. I got stuck on the Wikipedia page for Poland Springs reading about the natural spring in Maine where they'd been sucking water for over a hundred years independently until being bought out by Perrier in the '80s and then like, vicariously by Nestlé later on. I tapped the hyperlink for Nestlé. Largest international bottled water company. Subsidiaries: Acqua Panna, Arrowhead, Deer Park, Perrier, Poland Springs, San Pellegrino.

I swiped back to the old tab and changed the search again:
Abraham, Martin, San Francisco, Chronicle, Nestlé
The link was buried on like, the tenth page of search results under about a hundred archived articles on local dogs, traffic reports, and ads for water bubbler refills.
I tapped the hyperlink:
Don't Cry Over Spilled Blood–Kirk Gould
San Francisco Chronicle–'76

The headline loaded on *The Chronicle* website, but not the article.

There was a brief disclaimer instead:
In an effort to maximize available bandwidth and storage capacities, particular articles or issues may be physically archived.

Just fuckin' fine. I slapped the phone down on the bar and pounded the last of the beer. The bartender came over kind of hesitantly and took the empty bottle away.

"That gonna be it for the night," she implied.

Her name badge read: *Christine*, but I didn't call her by name.

People who wear name badges hate when you call them by name.

"Nah. Give me a drink. Whiskey. Straight. A double... please."

She reached for a tumbler on a shelf overhead.

"Jameson?"

"Sure."

"Long day?"

"Does it show?"

"Mostly long days sitting where you are."

"I thought it was something about all this..."

I waved a hand in the general vicinity of my worn-out self.

She smiled graciously. Like, my exact opposite, all sunny and smiling. Tall, stacked, blonde, and tanned. Made me question if the sultry cold weather hard-ass thing I was born into really worked for me as well as I thought. In general, I kept myself looking good. Veggies, cigs, and 40+ hours a week stocking baked beans will keep you pretty trim. My hair had like, no shape right now, and I never really have loved how dark it is, but it's fitting for an alabaster complexion, which was hardly ever threatened by mid-day UVs. Don't get me wrong, I do alright for myself, but a baggy sweater over tights and a half-way decent pair of boots passes for an east-coast guy's idea of a babe so long as she can hold her booze and knows at least three names of the Bruins' first shift that night.

"You got someone's attention." Christine pointed with her eyes to the other end of the bar where sat none other than the guy from the plane who wouldn't shut the fuck up the whole time.

"Oh, fuck me," I turned away.

"Uh oh."

"Of all the gin joints..."

"You know him?"

"I sat next to him on the plane out here."

"Makes sense. Half the out of towners from your flight are probably in the five hotel bars on this block."

"He wouldn't stop talking. I can't believe he's not talking right now. He's probably been all up and down the city talking to everybody, and now they're all avoiding him, so he had to come in here and find me."

"I think he's kind of cute."

He did adhere to the standard rules of attraction: fit, well dressed, clean, nice teeth, good skin.

"Easy on the eyes, rough on the ears."

She laughed.

"Want me to bill your room? You can sneak out of here?"

I risked a look in the guy's direction. He was like, straight up aware that we were talking about him, raised his glass in recognition.

"Ugh, no. Set us up. I'll humor the poor bastard."

She pulled down a couple new glasses.

"Hey buddy, how 'bout a drink," I offered down the bar.

He slid onto the stool beside me.

"I wasn't sure if you'd remember me."

"How could I not?"

"Was our time together that impactful?"

"Unforgettable, I'd say... no matter how much I tried."

He grinned in that like, humble way with his shoulders by his ears.

"Wontedly garrulous. A professional strength, a public failing."

"Wouldn't shut the fuck up, is what I kept thinking."

"Kept. Then I did stay on your mind?"

"Like a blood clot."

"What are we having?" Christine broke in.

I finished the Jameson.

"Something different. Gin and Tonic."

"Two," she asked.

The guy approved. She left the glasses condensating on the purply faux marble with a wink and bounced away. The tonic fizzed in a momentary lapse of interlocution.

"Here's looking at you." I was the first to drink.

He removed the wedge of lime from the edge of his glass and squeezed it into the gin. We were the only ones at the bar.

"First night in Indy," he observed.

"Ayuh."

"How are you liking it?"

"Everyone's been good to me. How about you?"

"Another go around. Most places, I spend more time in the airport than I do the city."

"Have you lighted on any new clients since we got in?"

"Not this afternoon."

"No illuminating prospects?"

"What?"

"Nothing. I thought you'd want to enlighten me if you did."

"Because of my job? Is that what you're saying?"

"Yes, you dick. I'm being funny. What the fuck."

"Sorry—I... it didn't make sense that you'd know."

"You're kidding? I could like, write your LinkedIn bio. Rick Parsons. Energy-efficient LED huckster from Washington state. Former marketing consultant for GE. Now you advise major corporations and office buildings on how to most efficiently update their lighting schematics with LED and take a percent of the energy-saving as commission."

"Wow."

"Not married. Doesn't have kids. Has a cat 'cause they can be left alone longer than dogs. Been to 48 states—all on business. The two states you haven't been to aren't Hawaii and Alaska... a common mistake."

"Alright, stop." He put his hands up like, I surrender.

"I got four hours of this."

"I still get nervous in the air."

"Four hours."

"I said it was a failing. At least I'm self-aware."

"I don't think it counts in retrospect."

"Past-self-aware then. Present-Me is a great judge of Past-Me, though not very influential over Future-Me."

"Future-Me... always getting Me into trouble."

"Nothing We can't handle."

A couple hours and several ounces of gin passed by.

Christine brought us the bill.

"You don't have to go home... but I do. So pay up and get the hell outta here."

"Charge it all to my room. You can tip," I told Rick, who was still reaching for his wallet.

While Christine rang us up, we had one of those silent conversations women can have that if you asked us about, we'd laugh and touch you on the shoulder and change the subject, but which we like, totally can and do in all kinds of situations of varying importance.

Christine: Everything alright?
Me: I'm okay. He seems nice.
Christine: I wrote my cell on your receipt just in case.
Me: Oh shit. Thanks.
Christine: Could be a creep. Gotta lookout for one another.
Me: I'm gonna text you right now so you have my number.

"... glad we ran into each other. It was fun talking to you." Rick was shouldering back into his suitcoat.

I put my phone away. Christine took the generous cash tip and waved good night. The track lighting dimmed overhead.

"You know what I wish we had?" I looked up at Rick.

"What's that?"

"Some weed. But I don't know anybody."

"You mean for right now?"

"I'm only here 'til morning... you figure it out."

A sausage vendor across the circle from the hotel sold foil-wrapped dimes from a backpack slung over the arm of his wheel-chair. I bought a Mexican Coke from the trash bag filled with ice in a cardboard box next to the grill.

We hung around watching the vendor rotate the meat on the cast iron grate. He chatted with us while serving the rest of the line.

"Today's the first day they ever walked to the bus alone. Usually, I go down there with 'em and wait at the bus stop, or I drive 'em down in the van if it's raining."

The vendor showed us a picture on his phone of two 4th grade-ish boys who stood eye level with the lens holding what appeared to be mostly empty backpacks.

"Good looking kids," Rick commented.

"They walk home every day after school without me... I don't know why it should make any difference if they do it in the morning, but it does."

I unpacked the tobacco from a cig, mixed some of it up with the weed from the dime, used a dollar bill to funnel it all back into the paper. We shared the spliff on the way back to my hotel room. The smoke clung to the humid Indiana night. Our fingers brushed against one another, groping for the filter as it passed.

My hands were on his chest. He held me by the hips. He tried to leave me in the lobby after we kissed.

"Wicked polite," I said, drawing him into a waiting elevator.

The sheets fit him better than his suit, outlining contours I had come to know in the dark, reclining in the over-plush Sheraton king-sized with his arms crossed behind his head.

I stood naked at the foot of the bed, still drying my hair from the shower. I could see him tracing my own outline with his eyes, sense memory recollection applying new layers to the collage of the past.

"Have you seen my phone," I asked him, crossing the room, peeking out the curtain. "It's getting light out."

"Here it is."

He pulled my phone out of the sheets.

I sat on the edge of the bed.

"Oh, God. It's past five."

"Good," he said, "I only have to be on a plane in three hours."

"Ugh."

A bunch of new notifications popped up, including a check-in alert for my flight home. I swiped away the copious alerts mindlessly—reminding myself for like, the billionth time to adjust my notification settings—but paused mid-swipe with the last banner slid hallway off the screen. I released my thumb, and the banner re-centered. I tapped the link to private messages on 23andme:

Notification–23andme–Yesterday:
New Private Message
From: Rose Amaranth
Message: do not go to San Francisco
I opened the chat dialogue box and typed: missed the funeral?

"Everything alright?" Rick was sitting up in the bed, casting around for his underwear.

"Yeah... I forgot to check-in for my flight."

"Who are you flying?"

"United."

"You'll be okay. Might want to do it now."

"I will."

He headed for the shower.

I put down the phone and got dressed. Before I pulled my shirt over my head, a new message alert vibrated.

RA: ??
RA: No Funeral
RA: Do not go to SF
Me: What's in SF?
RA: Do not trust Gould.
Me: and You?
RA: Don't go

"Wanna' share a car?" Rick called from the shower.

"Sure," I think I said.

"Don't order it yet. If we hurry, we can run up the block for a real cup of coffee first. We don't want to drink this hotel crap."

I wasn't responding.

The chatbox was still open, but:

Rose Amaranth has left the conversation...

2015 Los Angeles, CA

The right three lanes on the 101 are already jam-packed for a mile before the 405-South exit. Anxious commuters gas-breaking inches at a time between bumpers, leaving only three left-hand lanes open for Kirk Gould to change at neck-breaking speed. Other motorists swerve and dodge at the sight of the mismatched primer Mazda coupe encroaching on their rearview. Horns crescendo and fall. Breaks chirp and warble. Numerous well-timed merges aborted. OMW texts, traffic emojis, expletives.

Gould wears dark shades to cut the San Fernando solar arc bouncing off the rattling hood. He wants to catch up before Encino and get off the freeway before Thousand Oaks. Before the surface street grid is released from the city planning restrictions of urban development into generational wealth adjacent National Parks.

He picked out the vanity plate—BGPICTR—on the SLK-500 from a herd of semi-luxury vehicles making the 45 mile crusade from Hollywood to the suburbs. He followed close, leaving no gap to be slipped into by a Mini Cooper changing five lanes at a time under Barham Blvd, confident in the limited spatial awareness of the Mercedes driver. He fell behind when traffic came to a brief stand-still after Studio City and the Mercedes guy made a tricky move, using the Coldwater exit lane to gain a hundred yards before dipping back into the still moving flow of cars in the distance.

Even if the Mercedes guy was more aware of his surroundings, there would be no reason for him to suspect the geriatric pursuit of which he was currently the target. Hadn't done anything completely reprehensible as of late; no more evil in him than was expected of a studio executive. He was actually a pretty good guy outside of the professional milieu, good father, husband, tax-payer. Not the followed closely on the freeway type by any means.

Gould had nothing against the Mercedes guy. Never even met him. Never seen his face before today. Individual personal details weren't included in the target dossiers provided by the client. Make, model, year, color, condition, plate. No names, no VIN. Payment deposited to a Venmo account by a different user every time. Assignments arrived by hardcopy, unannounced, provided for minimal planning, and were required to be destroyed.

It beat the hell out of standing in front of the Office of the Registrar at the County Clerk's in Downey cherry-picking the next generation of independent hopefuls adding their names to the ledger for future extortion by the California Tax Commission. It was cheap to apply if you came with a plan, kept your head down, and followed the signs. Those who did had been warned. Ignored the beck of Gould's and others' call at the door, in the lot, waiting outside the bathroom. Saw their future peers and competitors fall prey to the consulting scam fees, which could net Gould a few hundred bucks a day when applied correctly.

"Registrar's office is right inside."

Gould opens the double glass door for a woman. Her hands are filled with loose paperwork. He recognizes the LLC formation applications, "Let me show you the way."

The woman stops, holds her documents against her chest.

"Back up, old man!"

"My office is upstairs in Publications 325 if you need any assistance after you file."

"I don't need any-fuckin' thing from you." The woman tosses her hair before walking confidently toward the registrar's office. Gould lets the door swing shut.

"They're getting tougher to hook," a fellow cheap suited consultant offers a cig. "It's Yelp ruining everything. They've been warned about you in a million negative reviews."

"Breaking my balls," Gould mutters through the smoke.

This guy couldn't even be sure Gould knew what Yelp was. The old man looked older up close. Tall and frail with wispy white hair—probably mostly bald—covered by a fedora to complete a Perry Mason suit that could have actually been worn by the historic litigator, judging by the threadbare condition.

The publications office upstairs was a front for washed-up journalists like Gould, who charged an exorbitant fee for the required business formation announcement that every new applicant must have printed in the local news within a few weeks of acceptance. Something that could be done at your local paper for $25 bucks.

If Gould still kept a regular eye over his shoulder instead of peering into the dregs of a dented silver flask, he might know this guy wasn't indeed a fellow publications consultant. Would have easily spotted him in a low-profile sedan at the far end of the lot the last few days. Could have followed him home and jimmied the lock the next time he was out, found the sparse binder comprised of his own background report, last know addresses, driving record, employment history, making him a perfect candidate for recruitment. No family. No assets. A withered nonagenarian who had already lived more life than he probably deserved. Impervious to threats, lawsuits, criminal charges, hospital bills, time, death.

With over 10 million residents rocketing around the 600ish mile racetrack of freeways connecting LA County daily, traffic accidents are as commonplace as Starbucks on the corner.

Good luck taking your insurance provider to another state after playing bumper cars on the San Diego Freeway for a few years. Never mind walking away from that three-year car lease. A couple early morning pileups before the fog clears on the way to Long Beach won't constitute a total loss, but you better believe when it comes time to trade-in, you'll either be buying whatever the dealer accredited shop Frankensteins back together or else humbly turning out your pockets to Honda for 36 months in the newest Civic without suffering a crippling down payment. Sure, there are some physics-defying saints of conveyance out there who've never heard the polymer crumple that comes after the moment of acceptance when you realize you've lost control—no dents, no dings, no coffee stains on the floorboards, no ash burns in the upholstery. Projected trade-in value concordant with the Blue Book for that year. But there were ways to deal with them.

It wouldn't be true to say that Gould was employed by a financing agency. Or even a dealer. All those nameless Venmo deposits would lead to what could best be called an interested fourth party if they could ever be tracked. A freelance consortium trading in persuasion. The kinds of guys known by a guy who knew a guy. Whatever your interests: corporate, political, personal; so long as there was money to be paid and eyes that could look the other way, there was no problem that couldn't be solved.

Gould was solving an issue as perpetual in the auto industry as any business: how to hold onto existing customers. Most financial institutions knew the best way—apply disproportionate interest to the value of a depreciating product. For car dealers, it had been easy. Leased, financed, or sold, once that Mercedes rolls off the lot, your investment is at their mercy. Over time, as the consumer became more savvy—accustom to Labor Day Sales-athon mailers and Owner Liability Agreements—the financier had to develop more creative ways to tip the scale in their direction. The result would be an inconsequential insurance claim, some cake in the pockets of the local dealer certified body shop, and a lessee trapped in a trade-in cycle which was difficult to escape without lump-sum payments or convoluted re-financing schemes.

Gould thinks of trade-ins as he drives. What he would trade, if he had it, and what for. In a way, he has already bartered so much.

Sacrificed, he thinks.

Over the years, he lost track of exactly what he was in it for. No matter what he reported, what was exposed, nothing changed. He once believed he could force redemption through a moral lens but could never draw focus long enough. After that, he thought with a gun but could never pull the trigger enough.

That didn't stop him from trying.

The Mazda engine reverberates off the median, humming through Sherman Oaks at 90mph. Traffic will open up after The

Galleria for a few miles before Topanga Canyon and Gould makes increasingly aggressive maneuvers to keep the Mercedes within a few cars at all times. Takes a long drag off the Marlboro, tasting the filter. Crushes the ember between two calloused fingers. Removes his sunglasses, an amber hue. He blinks through the windshield, adjusts the seatbelt across his chest—the airbag's been removed. A line of brake lights rolls downhill about a quarter-mile ahead. The slow-down progresses in stuttered waves. Gould lets off the gas before most, falls behind the Mercedes momentarily. He continues to coast as the brake-waves crash to a halt. The Mercedes gradually slows, unable to make any fancy maneuvers. Gould doesn't slam on the brake until he's within 25 feet. The Mazda shouldn't be going more than about 40mph on contact.

The smog is light today, permitting the sky to contrast the clouds whipped up into peaks. It hasn't rained in over a year, and the hills to the north are brown with black scars from previous fire seasons.

Don't Cry Over Spilled Blood
Gould, Kirk
SF Chronicle 1976

Dig your feet into the cool sand remaining on the bank
where the creek receded. The pail your mother sent you
with is cracked and broken and it's difficult to scoop up any
water. Hold the pail carefully, skimming the top where the
shallow stream is least murky. Run home as quickly as you
can. The brown water drips from the pail. Friends wave,
smiling, but you don't stop, hopping back and forth over the
drying riverbed, avoiding the loose refuse that didn't make
it to the landfill at the bottom of the hill.

A red candy foil flutters, caught like a flag on a dying
shrub: Kit-Kat, you know it says but don't know what it
means. Your Mother gave you a single piece once when the
aid workers brought clothes and supplies. They had white
skin but were good people and here to help. The cross they
wore was the symbol of their faith, same as the one over the
door to the house of worship they built before they left. The
supplies didn't last very long and no one ever mentioned if
there would be more.

Veer away from the river-bed before reaching the latrines which are being emptied in bucket-fulls. During the wet season it rained so hard the reservoir flooded and overflowed into the river. The rain washed everything away eventually, but the whole village smelled for a month. Since then, the old pit has been covered over with dirt and a new one was dug. The new reservoir is almost filled again and makes you want to hold your nose, but you have to use two hands to carry the pail. More than half the water remains when you arrive home.

Your mother adds to an already boiling pot over the small cooking fire. She smiles and holds out her hand for you to take. She's been weak since your sister was born. She says having a baby is very difficult and she'll be better soon. But you notice she always gives you more to eat than herself, and sometimes, she doesn't eat at all. She says that's why she can't feed your sister and needs to give her the formula powder she sends you to purchase once a week when a crowded van goes into the nearby town. She always gives you a short list, and the formula is always on it. The store sells a lot of things, but the formula is most expensive. The money you have could buy much more: meat, eggs, potato, leafy greens, a piece of fruit, a gallon of water. Instead you buy a bag of beans, a bag of rice, and a can of Gerber: Good Start...

...a back-up signal wakes you before the sun can find the holes in the sheet you've hung over the east-facing window. The moving trucks have been coming more frequently. Or you've noticed them more. The whole neighborhood has turned over in the last year. The families you knew growing

89

up, long gone. The job market suffering for years, leveled by Wal-Mart and McDonald's.

Steady migration from LA County drove up housing to Executive-and-higher ranges starting around the lake, eventually creeping out of the forest and into town. Rent was increased where it could be, property taxes rose to accommodate for the refined interests of the middle-class. Developers made deals with property owners to extricate the last of the holdouts. Lease agreements were bought out for less than the going cost of first and last month's.

Katrina took the kids to your in-laws when you wanted to wait for a better offer. They packed the most important belongings. Since then, you've sold off the rest in order of necessity: washer, dryer, furniture, refrigerator, air conditioner, television.

The wood floor is cool like the desert it was built on. Before noon, daylight on the stucco walls will turn the empty home into an oven. Better to go sit out in the driveway with the last of your possessions. Mr. Torrio, from two houses down, stops by to tell you he's done packing up and so long. He and his wife took the modest buy-out as a sign of change. Cashed in a couple of long-term savings accounts with a minimal penalty, retired a couple years early, and bought a condo in Arizona outside of Mesa. Not with the nest egg they'd set out for, but close. Both in good health. With some smart planning and a little luck, they'll be just fine. He doesn't ask about Katrina or the boys, but the way he keeps looking past you at the sheet-curtained windows makes you think he wants to. He wishes you well before leaving for good.

With the Torrios gone, you're the last on the block, one of three occupied properties in the whole neighborhood. You've seen how it happens in other parts of town. The day the flatbeds arrive to deliver the bulldozers is the last chance you'll get. They park in the street overnight, security guards positioned to protect the faded yellow monsters chained to the freight deck. In the morning, demolition will start whether you've made a deal or not. You could refuse to leave; stand in the doorway, braced in the frame. Breathe the dust of family life drifting from the rubble.

You didn't get angry when the town started to change, thought a little prosperity would be good for everyone. It wasn't watching the local stores close, or the new developments being built. Or having to drive the kids to a new school, or that your voting precinct had been changed. What set you off was when you realized how much the water bill increased in the last few years. Why should you pay for a sustentative utility when they've been sucking it out of the lake by the ton for a hundred years? They can't afford to pump a little downhill?

You found the city planning schedule and attended the meetings but never spoke up. Something about the way issues were discussed diminished your outrage to apathy. City officials were aware of the increased cost of living, expanding commercial zoning, redistricting, unrest, but chalked them up to conditions of progress. Sacrifices for the greater good.

After all, the bottling plant brought in a good deal of revenue—was practically a part of the town, a member of the community.

Katrina's parents have offered their guest house until you can get on your feet again. You've stalled as long as possible, but soon the last of the appliances will be sold, and you'll have no excuse to not accept their charity. Katrina says it doesn't matter if you're struggling now, that you'll get through it together. Says her parents love having the kids there. Besides, it's only temporary.

It's not pride that holds you back, you tell yourself, lying on the wood floor at night, it's principle. You deserve to live in a place where the community supports itself, holds people up when they're down. It's why your parents came here, why you brought two sons into the world: faith in the system, in goodwill, the impossible dream.

The unemployment benefits you've received since being laid off will expire at the end of the month. You've called up old friends looking for work, supervisors, cousins, but nothing's come through. There's only one place anyone's heard of that's hiring. They always are. Tomorrow you'll call the landlord and accept the lease buy-out. After that, you'll take the bus up to the lake and apply at the Arrowhead bottling plant…

These two seemingly unrelated stories of human interest from across the globe may, to the Sunday reader with slippered feet warming on a hassock before the fire, not appear to have any common thread binding their seam together.

A young boy in an African country deemed underdeveloped by a corporate structure uninterested in aiding beyond measures aimed at the region's valuable natural resources, struggling to feed his family.

A first-generation American, slipping daily from the dream his parents risked their lives through jungle, and rebellion, and bandits, and borders to provide access to. Desperate to maintain little more than shelter provided by the fruits of his own merit. Crushed by an economy favoring industry over humanity. Grandfathering profitable access to federal land but not clean and affordable drinking water for the public whose tax dollars pay to maintain it.

Though not the first to employ the tactic, this offense pattern has been common practice for the better part of a century by Nestlé: strip vital natural resources, exploit the population dependent on those resources, and redistribute those resources back to the population for a profit. Unashamed marketing campaigns in Maine, Michigan, California.

You need water, clean water, not water from a filthy pipe; water from the ground, our ground, through our pipes. Trust us. It's not like you were using it. Like your ancestors thrived by it. It's not like you can taste the blood of the people who never owned anything, who settled this land and prayed for it and worshiped every molecule before the word existed, we filtered it too well. Shipped by glass-lined tankers to preserve the rich, natural elements. From our land to your lips—but not to Nigeria, to Malawi, to the Congo where the oil from Anglo vessels poisoned a great wonder of the world. They don't need water. They need nutrients, sustenance, vitality. Not the milk of mother's breast, that tap runs dry. A fresh start. A good start. Trust us, we vacuum sealed it.

Not close enough to home? The case is the same down

the street on Russian Hill. The upper-middle-class wannabe socialite convinces themselves what they've attained sets them apart from the struggling masses: copious possessions, modest education, imported vehicle, color TV, microwave oven. Interest payments. Student debt. Finance charges. Condo owner's association dues. Name brands. Appearances. Popular opinion would agree. What could be more enjoyable than a cool beer in front of a color TV in your own home, comfortable in the knowledge that the mortgage payment isn't due for another three weeks.

The truth is, for a majority of the population, the difference between have and have-not is in a couple month's bills. So says Victoria Miller, a certified Mother Craft nurse, tasked with the responsibility of informing new mothers of the Nestlé recommended best practices, "...*you can feel it...desperate... desperation in people all over the city...I'm at homes in all different neighborhoods, and I see it. New parents, single mothers... all different income levels, when they hear the cost of the formula and the bottles, all the extra stuff they're supposed to buy along with it... they know they can't afford another bill, couldn't afford the take-out food sitting in bags on the counter, but they want to provide, they think it's best for their baby...I tell them it is... it's my job.*"

But surely, you'd ask, Mrs. Miller has come across a family with disposable income, the means to care for their own? After all, we do live in one of the most prosperous and costly cities in the world. We know they exist, those in the financial minority with access to doctor-recommended organic vegetables, clean drinking water, and arguably the most valuable asset of all, time. What of them, Mrs. Miller?

"They breastfeed."

We reached out to Mrs. Miller's Bay Area supervisor, Martin Abraham, for comment. Mr. Abraham's office failed to return our request...

2015 San Francisco, CA

I minimized the window, hiding the digitized scan of the article. The basement of *The Chronicle* was filled with the paranoia that followed me since I left Indianapolis. Rows of decommissioned microfiche machines stretched into the darkness of the expansive archive stack. Coincidence lost the novelty of innocence, started adding up to like, intent. In the stiff-necked, dry-mouthed, so hung-over quiet of an early morning flight from IND to SFO, the feeling crept in that I knew better than to ever open an unsolicited package on my doorstep. Shouldn't have balked routine. Routine served me well. Had netted job security, a savings account, respectable Blu-ray collection. So I didn't know my ancestors... big fuckin' deal. They had been alive, they did some things—maybe not all of them admirable, probably some less than holy, not bad, not good, and now dead. But then why was I here? And why was I like... here...

Rose Amaranth was right.
I'd have to choose not to go to San Francisco.
I made it all the way to departures. Rick was already in the air,

off to hock cost-effective luminosity to the rest of the Midwest.

Final boarding was being called for United 3514 as I got to the gate. I juggled over my license and ticket to the boarding attendant who scanned, checked, re-scanned, and re-checked.

"I'm sorry, but you have the wrong flight. You want flight 1450 down at gate 37B. If you hurry, you can still make it."

"Oh, thanks," I told her, taking back my identification.

I had only gone a few steps when the boarding attendant's voice crackled through the intercom.

"This is the last call for final boarding, Flight 3514 Indiana to Boston."

I stopped, looked at the ticket in my hand, and went back.

"Sorry, did you say this was the flight to Boston?"

"Yes, ma'am. I did."

"That's my flight."

"No, your flight is 1450 down at gate 37B, remember?"

"But look," I showed her my ticket. She retook the ticket, scanned it, checked it, spun her computer monitor in my direction.

"See, Jo Burke, Flight 1450, Indianapolis to San Francisco."

"The hell?"

"Sorry, Ms. Burke. If you hurry, you can still catch it. Let me–"

She spun her monitor, prodded the touch screen in a couple places, and held her hand out for a fresh ticket from a printer on her pedestal. I watched as she tore up my old boarding pass and handed me the new one.

"Have a great day, Ms. Burke."

"Yeah," I said, but she was already announcing her next flight.

I did have time to make it if I hurried and boarded as they were getting ready to seal the cabin door.

"How'd it go," the kid working the reception desk asked when I came out the steps leading up from the archive.

"Just fine."

"Did you find what you were looking for?"

"I'm not sure... hey listen, did anyone else go down there after me?"

He looked around the empty lobby, "You're the first person that's asked me anything the whole time I've worked here."

"How long's that been?"

"About a week."

"Anybody call asking about obituaries? Or old *Chronicle* writers?"

"We don't get a lot of phone calls, not as much as we used to. That's what they told me, at least. Have you tried Googling it?"

"I'll have to try that..." I reached for my smokes, headed for the exit.

"Well, but wait," the kid called out, "oh man, I'm supposed to have like, a directory," he clicked around anxiously on the reception computer, "they showed me how to find it."

"The guy I'm looking for's long gone. Thanks anyway, kid."

I left.

The first ash hadn't fallen off the Marlboro when the kid came running out. He handed me a torn note on *Chronicle* letterhead.

"That's the name and number of the head editor. He's been here forever... if you're looking for someone, he'd know them."

"Thanks, kid. I'll give him a call."

"Can you mention I was helpful? Like, a helpful receptionist..."

"Okay."

98

"And tell him I have a BA in creative writing... UC Berkeley... if it comes up."

"Any special skills you want me to list?"

"Huh?"

"Forget it. I'll tell him."

"Thanks, thank you. Tell him Danny, Danny Smith."

"Thanks, Danny," I told him as he slipped back inside.

The biggest favor I could do the kid was to not bring his name up at all. Naive transparency wasn't a great line of defense against solicitation. Pretty sure it didn't get you very far in the newspaper business at all.

"Your dime."

It was hard to hear his voice over the bullpen noise on the other end of the line.

"Curtis Donavan?"

"You got him."

"I'm looking for a writer."

"We don't give out employee information."

"I don't think he's still an employee."

"You can try payroll. Or records. They might have something."

"You only have one article of his in the archives, and it's from '76. Would payroll be able to help with that?"

"Guess not. What's the guy's name anyway?"

"Kirk Gould."

He didn't respond right away. A door slammed. The noise of the bullpen quieted.

"Kirk Gould isn't employed here."

"Yeah. I know. That's why I'm calling you."

"I wasn't even here in the '70s."

"But you've been there longer than most?"

"Close to 25 years."

"You do know Kirk Gould?"

A pause, "I know the name."

"And something else..."

"What paper are you with?"

"I'm not."

"You're a private investigator?"

"No."

"Insurance?"

"I'm a fuckin' grocery manager at a Stop & Shop. I got no like, ulterior motives. I'm not trying to screw anybody here, man. I'm looking for this guy Gould. You either know him, or you don't. You got nothing to say? That's just fine. Forget I asked."

"Stop & Shop?"

"Yeah."

"Whereabouts?"

"Saugus."

"No shit. I grew up in Lynn."

"City of sin."

"Fuckin' A. I'd really like to help you but the name's all I know and it's been a long time since I heard it."

"Whatever then..."

"Look, if I hear anything. I'll give you a ring."

"Yeah, right. Don't bother. I don't think I'm sticking around."

"You're the one asking questions. You don't want answers?"

The fog drifted over the bay on the south side of Embarcadero

Boulevard. Only a few blocks, but a world away from the high-dollar shops and tourist cruises closer to the Golden Gate, the Bay Bridge loomed over squat concrete and red brick warehouses. Docks of private sailboats creaked and rubbed at their moorings below the saltwater cloud cover.

I smoked, waiting for Donavan on a city bench outside a burger and beer shack called Red's Java House. He asked to meet here, said we should talk in person. Not like I had anywhere to be. He could have his Orson Welles moment, appearing from the fog to lecture me about penicillin and cuckoo-clocks. Some aging desk editor who'll use any whiff of a story as an excuse to get out of the office. Though something about the way his voice changed made me wonder. Something he heard and didn't like. A reminder of a past you thought you'd outlived, wouldn't need to reconcile, calling you up at work and generally fucking up your day.

He didn't appear from out of the fog, was there all along. Dressed like a Silicon Valley retiree: t-shirt, jeans, Birkenstocks, and fuckin' socks. Not what I pictured when I thought, big-city news editor. Had been watching from the patio furniture dining area outside Red's, working on a chili cheese dog with fries, sipping a beer from a plastic cup. By the time my periphery made note, the fries were half gone. When he knew I was aware of him, he motioned with his hand for me to come over. He nudged an empty chair with his toe, and I took the invitation to have a seat.

"Want something? Food's good."

"That's alright." I eyed the hot dog.

"You a vegetarian?"

"Mostly."

"They got fish."

"Really, it's fine."

He held out the thatched plastic tray of fries, half of which were now chili-fied. I picked out a dry one and munched it.

"Beer," he offered next.

"Why not."

"Hey Red!" He yelled through the shack screen door, leaned into me, "His name's not really Red, pisses him off," leaned back smiling to himself.

"The hell you want," came through the screen door.

"Couple of beers!"

The beers were brought out in more plastic cups. Donavan finished his dinner. I lit up and offered him a smoke.

"No thanks, those things will kill you."

"Here's to what won't," I raised my cup in his direction.

We drank.

"First time in SF?"

"Yup."

"How's things back east?"

"Bleak."

"It can seem that way, I know."

"Is that why you left?"

"I left because there wasn't anything left for me there. Print work in that town's wicked competitive. Close to New York, DC, there's a lotta pressure to run with the big dogs, you gotta be scrappy. Big dogs eat first and last. There's not a lot in between. Feel me?"

"How'd you know things would be different out here?"

"I didn't. I was running out of prospects and got offered a favor, a recommendation from an old-timer..."

"Gould?"

"Our mutual variable."

"So, you do know him."

"More like, knew of him... or he knew of me."

"When's the last time you saw him?"

"I never have."

"Never seen him in person?"

"Only ever spoken to him once over the phone. Only heard his name once before that."

"When?"

"Long time. Around the time your old man..."

"Yeah..."

"Sorry... I saw him that day..."

"I don't remember you."

"You were so young."

"Yeah, but I remember. I was with him every day in the hospital until he died. Me and my Ma, sometimes only me."

"He never made it to the hospital. I saw the police report, the death certificate."

"Police report?"

He unlocked his phone and started scrolling. Found what he was looking for and spun the screen around on the table. A picture of an old *Boston Herald* article. Not a ton of information. A Charlestown shooting back in '90. Four dead. Three unidentified. One Boston local, veteran, widower, survived by Grandfather, Grandmother, daughter...

"You remember this?"

"No... I thought you meant my dad, my adoptive dad..."

"You mean Joe Sr.?" Donavan makes a puzzled face.

"I guess so."

"That's your dad's grandfather. Your old man was raised by his grandparents... Joe Sr. never told you any of this?"

"They told me I was adopted, an orphan, from Worcester."

"Worcester State? That place is a fuckin' nuthouse."

"That's what I said."

A notification dinged on my phone.

"Sent you that article," he said.

I looked at my phone. The article popped up in a text thread—another picture text-bubbled in: an old Polaroid taken in a jungle setting. Two young guys in sleeveless army greens, M-16 rifles at their sides, smoke rising from behind palm trees in the distance. They posed for the photo but didn't smile. Someone had written with Sharpie in the Polaroid border:

Donavan–Burke–Grenada–'84

"The year I was born."

"Your mother was pissed. Bad enough we were stationed out of state on reserves half the year, but a hot war, another people's war, while she waited in Litchfield with you and Joe Sr..."

"You knew her?"

"We all grew up together, Evie and Joe and me. I never got a chance to say goodbye. By the time I was discharged... she was already gone, and your old man was... he didn't take it well."

"You said you saw him that day. You were there?"

"No."

"But you were involved?"

"No way. Joe and I weren't as close then. We were always friends... he was a good guy but... unpredictable. I'd throw him a gig every here and there when I needed a little extra weight for a story and scruples were in question. The last time we saw each other, someone had been asking around, got in touch with *The Herald*, and found me. I got a third-hand message for him and passed it on... a time and place... a few blocks from where it happened. He didn't know I read the note before I gave it to him, maybe he assumed. That was the first time I ever heard of Kirk Gould."

"Did Gould kill him?"

"I never thought so... they found them bleeding out together. Never identified the other shooters."

"Did you do anything about it? Did you try to find out what happened?"

"I was losing my footing at *The Herald*. Didn't have the sway it takes to push any kind of angle. Besides, I was questioned by The Finest a handful of times. Can't write about a murder if you're a suspect. Got my service record combed through, family interviewed, surrendered years of unrelated research materials."

"You said he gave you a recommendation?"

"Years later. Mid-'90s. I get a call, and it's a guy saying he's Kirk Gould. Says Boston's washed up and that *The Herald's* a bullshit tabloid and all the real action's out west. Says he can get me an editor's desk gig at *The Chronicle*. Says he owes me one. One for what, I ask him. He says, for ever getting me involved."

"And you what, ignored the implication?"

"I wasn't in a position to take any moral high road. He wasn't wrong about Boston either. If you weren't in tech or real estate at the time, next best bet was to pound sand. My knuckles were raw, my savings were gone. Even with references... in those days, it was even tougher for a Black man to find an apartment outside of Roxbury or fuckin' Lynn, and no one even did you the favor of pretending otherwise. He must have known... Gould... knew I was down and out. Waited until I was alone, bored, desperate, broke... willing... that's when he called on me... when he called on Joe... could be that's why he called you..."

"Gould's never actually got in touch with me."

"Then why the hell are you here?"

"Ever heard the name Abraham?"

"Martin Abraham?"

"You know him?"

"Gould wrote about him," he confirmed.

"Yeah. The only story of his on file."

Donavan finished the last of his beer in a gulp, "The data transfer was a cluster fuck. A lot of good stuff didn't make it to the new system. If you fired up the old microfiche you might find something."

"It's tough to find any info on Kirk Gould... even with a background check."

"Supposedly he went to LA after *The Chronicle*. But, it's been so long..."

"Tougher to find anything on Abraham. No known addresses, previous employers, no obituary. In Gould's article, it says that Abraham had something to do with baby formula?"

"Obituary?"

"Abraham's. He's dead."

"No shit."

"Saw his grave..."

I had never heard a gunshot before. I thought a ship snapped a tie line down on the dock. I reached across the table to touch Donavan's hand. His face turned into a pained mask. His skin was already cold, getting pale—no time for breathless last words. Blood diffused across his chest, down his shirt front. His body started to tilt from the waist up. I leaned across further—as if I could actually hold him up—but he slipped out of my grasp. His face smacked into the patio table before his dead weight shifted, buckling the legs and taking us both to the ground.

Another gunshot, flat, disconnected, dug into the pavement a few inches from my head. Bits of tar scraped my cheeks.

"Don, what the fuck you doin' man?" Red was shouting.

Me and Donavan were eye to eye. He stared with that same pained mask. Blood oozed in a puddle from under his chin. I rolled over onto my side. A bullet thumped behind me. I got to my feet and hauled ass across the street into an alleyway. Another gunshot echoed from behind.

I ran out the alley on the next block and almost knocked a guy over when I crashed into him. The cellphone went flying out of his hand. His briefcase clunked to the ground and popped open. Pens rolled into the street. Papers blew away. Product samples smashed when they fell, littering the sidewalk with shards of energy-efficient LED.

2015 Los Angeles, CA

The terrain transformed as we floated overhead.
Rolling farmlands, desert, city, beach, the outstretched Pacific.

We shuttled to a car rental place down the street. The LAX palm tree landscaping ended after a quarter-mile, and we were on Century Blvd. Eight lanes of fast food, gas stations, and airport branches of popular hotels. This place isn't included in any smash cut Disney promos. No bespoke tailors or designer brand shops to be found. Like any neighborhood surrounding an airfield, this was a bland, underdeveloped, billboard adorned, industrial, parking-lotted port of entry meant to be utilized briefly then forgotten. Where the county pulled out of revitalization, so the streets that don't lead to terminals are a little more narrow than they should be. The part of town you buy a house in when you really can't afford one. The district's been declared historic, stunting growth, marginalizing inhabitants. *For Lease* signs hang in every other door and each other one's a family-owned restaurant. The kind of place you find a Woolworth's and you think, Woolworth's? I thought they shut down. But you see people wandering in and out, so you figure you must be wrong.

I stood outside of FOX Car Rentals, smoking while Rick picked up his reservation. Traffic sped to and from LAX. Blinker-less last-ditch efforts to make the lane for departures, the on-ramp for the 405, the drive-thru for some burger place called Carl's Jr.

I watched starry-eyed tourists from all over the world fold up their rental agreements, gaze questioningly at the gas prices of the Chevron across the street—almost five bucks a gallon—and wait anxiously for their Dodge Caravan to be wheeled around. What were they gonna do? Take the bus? Hollywood's more than 10 miles away, and Maps says it could take over an hour to get there with traffic.

"Can I get one of those?" A Bum was hanging his arms through the bars of the metal railing separating FOX from the sidewalk. I handed him the pack of Marlboros. He took one, lit it, and handed back the rest.

He didn't look like a bum, had on new sneakers, a new wind-breaker, but that didn't stop him from asking, "Hey, look, I came down here to visit my girl at work on her birthday. It's her birthday today, you know? And I didn't want to like, ask her cause of it being her birthday and all, but I don't have the cash to get the bus back to the East Side." He held out his hand. In it, some coins and a couple wrinkled dollar bills, "Think you could help me out? I'm trying to put together enough for the bus."

I found a buck stuffed down in my back pocket and handed it over, with plenty of eye-rolling and smoke blowing to let him know I wasn't thrilled about it.

He took the bill but said, "That's it? The bus is like, $6.50 to

Eagle Rock."

"Up yours, buddy. I gave you the fuckin' buck, didn't I?"

"Oh shit! Okay, alright. I feel you. Not to be fucked with, I like that."

"Then why you still doing it?"

"Woah! I was like, acknowledging your position, right?"

A Pedestrian walked by smoking a butt. The Bum held up two fingers at the guy, the Pedestrian stopped, got out his pack, and handed over a cig, disregarding the one already lit in his beneficiary's hand. The Pedestrian moved along. The Bum tucked the fresh smoke behind his ear. He smiled at the look on my face.

"Sucker born every minute," I told him.

"What time did you pop out?"

"Yeah, sure. Me included."

"Then why the front?"

"Never cared much for begging."

He clicked his tongue, "Girl, shit... we in LA. It ain't begging. That's the hustle."

A chime dinged. The Bum pulled out his iPhone. Started responding to a text, holding the cig on his lip. When he stopped, "That's the homie, gotta bounce."

"Okay."

"Yo," he said, reaching into his pocket, "no hard feelings."

He tossed a green plastic cylinder up over the railing. I caught it and looked inside: a pre-rolled joint about the size of my finger.

"Say hello to Hollywood for me."

We had been on the road for close to an hour and weren't anywhere near the Kingsley, and Fountain, and Prospect, that

Wilder loved to showcase so frequently. Near where Philip Marlowe stayed in a little rented bungalow. Up the street from the same Chinatown where Jack had to, *forget it, Jake*. Instead, we were headed north on surface streets, avoiding the 405, which Rick explained was a parking lot at this time of day.

"Light it up," he told me as we passed signs for The Getty Center, a concrete sculpture of a museum built up high into the canyon walls.

He rolled the Chrysler windows down, pulling the hot afternoon in around us. Primrose and pine, sage, dirt. The pot wasn't great but there was a lot of it. The radio crackled when we came to the top of the canyon, breaking up the call letters for KJAZZ, "Only station in town worth listening to."

The next tune that came in was a real moody soundtrack by Miles Davis that I recognized. We passed Mulholland drive, and Rick caught me staring.

"Check that out..." he pointed as we rounded the last turn before the incline.

A city spread out between us and the next mountain range, miles away. Cut in half lengthwise by a couple freeways. Flat, low, sun-bleached, shimmering in the heat; the San Fernando Valley, stretching from here to the coast.

"We'll go into Hollywood later," Rick told me.

He had a few pitches to make someplace called Sun Valley. A cinder block manufacturer and some pipe fitting warehouse or something.

"Not very exciting, sorry. I could drop you off somewhere?"

"Nah. I feel safer with you."

He rolled up the window. The joint was cashed.

"I still think you should file a report."

"I just want to go home." I was already scrolling through Orbitz.

We passed Ventura Blvd and headed back inland when signs started popping up for Panorama City. The desert fought to reclaim the aging suburbs. Lawns choked by sand. Dated architecture, stucco eroding. Vast shopping centers where only the Sears and Vallarta are still in business. Fast food, auto body, strip club, liquor store. The last street on the grid. A couple more underpasses and regular traffic was replaced by 18-wheelers.

Residential gave way to industrial. The desert resumed its empire at the foothills between us and the next valley.

I hadn't received any 23andme messages. Whoever it was that dragged me out here didn't seem too concerned anymore—and if I'm the one to blame, then it's still true, and I'm sorry I ever got involved.

"... some of my favorite places have closed over the last few years, but something new is always coming around. Each time I'm in town, I find a new favorite..." Rick was talking, "Funny how at some point we decided to always move forward, you know? No more ruins. Knock it down and plaster it over. I mean, I get it... industrial revolution, low-cost fabrication, synthetics. In the name of progress, all that. It's like, by the time people got out here, they said, slap something up for the night, and we'll fix it tomorrow... you sure you're alright?"

We slowed to a stoplight.

"Just fine," I answered but wasn't listening.

My attention was stuck on the side-view mirror.

Rick glanced in the rearview but didn't have time to react.

A Ford Fiesta with a smashed-up front end was scraping through the two lanes of cars behind us. Drivers cranked their wheels, inching forward, but couldn't avoid being gouged up on one whole side of their paint job. The rusty Fiesta wasn't slowed by the friction and hit our rear bumper hard. The passenger airbag knocked the wind out of me. I sucked deep breaths. Choked on the cornstarch filling the cabin. Before the airbag fully deflated, we were rocked again by the Fiesta mangling itself along the driver's side exterior. I rolled my window down to clear the air and caught a glimpse of the Fiesta taking a yellow left-turn light at the intersection.

"Mother fuck! He's running away!"

I turned to Rick, but he was passed out cold from the impact of the airbag. An imprint of his wristwatch visible on his forehead.

Stunned drivers were gradually getting out of their cars to survey damage. No one was trying to stop the Fiesta from getting away. A couple ran up from the sidewalk waving at me like, are you okay? I nudged Rick, but he didn't move, so I shoved him and swung my left leg over the cup holders to his side. I kicked his feet away and stepped on the gas. Perpendicular traffic resumed at the intersection. I fishtailed into the stream through the red left-turn light.

The Ford hadn't made it far past the intersection by the time I straightened the Chrysler out, managed to stay in a lane with minimal drifting, approaching 60mph quickly on the industrial roadway. The Fiesta was forced to slow at the next intersection but jumped into oncoming traffic through another red light. I whipped the Chrysler to the far-right side of my lane and bounced two tires up onto the curb, riding the concrete to the crosswalk.

I laid on the horn, cutting the wrong way under the stoplight.

I heard the collision but didn't look to see what happened.

The Fiesta was gaining speed again, weaving around slower vehicles. I was able to keep up with a few green lights on my side. Rick started to shift into consciousness when the Chrysler bounced over a set of railroad tracks. We passed signs for Bob Hope Airport. The Fiesta took the last side-street before the airfield. I followed, gunning the engine on the narrow road, catching the Fiesta, and bumping the back hatch with the Chrysler's grill. The Fiesta wobbled but didn't lose control, stayed on the road until it ended in a cul-de-sac. The driver skidded to a stop, forcing me to brake hard enough to send Rick forward against his seat belt.

"What's the matter," he mumbled.

I pulled myself back over to my side of the car and opened the door, stood half out with my arm resting on the roof. An old man—like, really old—got out of the motionless Fiesta.

"Crazy asshole! You coulda killed somebody," I shouted.

He didn't respond, started shuffling over to us.

"You have insurance and everything?" I asked him. "Probably doesn't even have his license," I leaned in and told Rick, who still wasn't totally aware.

The old man approached the driver's side door.

"It's all in his name, but he's gonna need a second. You okay? You have insurance and everything," I repeated.

The old bastard could have been in shock. He didn't respond, reached into the front pocket of his overcoat for what I assumed was his paperwork. What he pulled out was a short revolver, which he pointed at the driver's side window. Inside the car, Rick was waking up and processing the reality of the old man.

"Shit," was all he got time for.

The revolver went off, busting the window with the first round before driving into Rick's chest. Two more shots followed through the window frame. Rick's body shuddered from the impact but didn't move again.

I couldn't think of anything to say. I stood there watching the second person of the day bleed out in front of me.

The old man leaned in the broken window and took Rick's cell phone from inside the blood-stained suit jacket. He put the gun away and tore the phone case off. Using a paper clip, he removed the SIM card tray from the phone's side. Tossed the SIM card on the ground and crushed it with his heel. Powered the phone off and threw it over the chain-link fence separating us from the airfield. A flight tore in for a landing, bending perimeter tree-tops along in the turbulence wake.

The old man looked at me across the Chrysler, "Got a phone?"

"You gonna smash it?"

He reached out an open hand, "Let me have it."

I held my iPhone out to him.

"No pass code," he condescended.

I shrugged.

He took the phone and swiped through the home screens. None of my apps were in folders. He turned the phone around so I could see.

"Last app on that page. Recognize it?"

"Nah," I didn't.

He highlighted the unknown app and deleted it. Swiped some more. Turned the phone back to me.

"Recognize the profile name?"

"No."

"Ever grant access to a configuration profile?"

"Umm... no."

He deleted the profile, handed back the phone, and started rifling through Rick's dead pockets.

"You knew this guy?"

"For a minute."

"Where'd you meet?"

"On a flight..."

"Knew his name?"

"Rick."

"Why are you in LA?"

"Hey. Look, man. I know you aren't a cop or whatever, so I'm answering these questions of like, my own volition..."

"Okay."

"I came here looking for someone."

"You want to tell me who?"

"Not yet."

"Did you know you were being followed?"

"By who?"

He found what he wanted and tossed me Rick's wallet.

"Open it," he told me.

I opened the wallet. There wasn't much inside: some cash—no receipts, a Massachusetts driver's license with Rick's picture but not his name, a reloadable Visa. No second form of identification. The old man found a huge automatic pistol under the bloody suitcoat. He wiped it down with the flap of his jacket and threw it into the woods. I handed back the wallet when he motioned for it. He took the ID out and tossed the rest on the ground.

"He installed a tracking app on your phone. It's like a child safety thing. That's how he followed you. Probably was seeing any texts or messages too."

"How can you even be sure it was him?"

"Did you meet anyone else on your way out here?"

"A few people."

"Anyone get as close as he did?"

"What the fuck is that supposed to mean?"

"Means he's the one that did it."

"I met Donavan in San Francisco. He's dead."

Gould didn't say anything. Lit a smoke.

"I found Abraham, too. In Indiana. I was the only one at his funeral."

"Why are you telling me?"

"You're Kirk Gould."

He started walking away, "Get in the car."

"I'm not going any fuckin' where with you."

"Stay here then. You can help the cops find his gun."

Gould took us through Burbank into Glendale, where he ditched the Fiesta at a junkyard behind a strip club. He paid cash for some beater Dodge Neon. It was getting late by the time we drove away. The blinding sunset turned the horizon purple, and though the day wouldn't succumb to the night for another couple hours, the eastern hillside at our backs was already cast in shadow.

This part of the city remained semi-industrial beneath the freeways and through the suburbs. The Hollywood I imagined was still nowhere to be found. The un-uniqueness of city life proceeded up the side streets, a laundry mat, CVS, like anywhere else.

I could have asked Gould if he was the one who sent the DNA kit. Who was Abraham? Did he know the name Rose Amaranth? Had he known my family? Did he really call me out here like Donavan had said? Had he done the same to my father? Is that why he was dead? Something told me we wouldn't be here if the answer wasn't what I thought it was.

Instead, after minutes of road chewing silence...

"Where are we going?"

Gould didn't answer right away.

He drove the little sedan with his knees. Pulled out a dented silver flask and unscrewed the lid. Drank. Handed me the flask, which smelled like something I never smelled before. I took a small swig and went back for a second. Gould lit a couple Marlboro Lights and handed me one.

"We're going to a lab a couple miles from here."

"What kind of lab?"

"A lab. A testing lab."

"Testing what?"

"All kinds of shit, but what else do you think?"

"Water."

"Smarter than you look, kid."

"I thought the Nestlé thing was out at Lake Arrowhead."

"This is some third-party analysis lab. They run tests for the state, for hospitals, and yeah... for Nestlé."

"If there's something wrong with the water, won't the lab report it?"

"Don't you get who you're dealing with? Did you see the piece that guy was carrying you were driving around with? You know where you were headed before I intervened?"

I tried not to think of the ditch Rick planned to unceremoniously fill with my voided remains. "Yeah. Well, that's like, one guy."

"And Donavan before that," he reminded, "others too..."

"Why now then? If this has been going on since the '70s?"

"Before that."

"Fine! The last hundred years then. Why now? The baby formula thing wasn't enough? Incorporating public land isn't enough? Kit-Kats, whatever the fuck that's got to do with anything... that isn't enough? Not enough you got my old man killed... got me being hunted down—shot at and shit. That's all not enough? You don't think if people cared, they'd be paying attention already?"

Gould let me finish without interrupting. He puffed calmly on the Marlboro, eyes on the road.

"Ever heard of polyfluoroalkyl substances," he asked after a quiet moment.

"No."

"You've heard of BPA, though?"

"In plastic bottles or something?"

"They're called forever chemicals. They leech into ground-water, soil, animals, your blood."

"And it's bad for you?"

"I'm telling you the shit they use to keep Big Mac grease from soaking through the paper wrapper is bumping elbows with your DNA."

"I don't really eat fast food."

"Fuckin' organic, wheatgrass fed, free-range, ethical cow shit grown strawberries then. You buy those?"

"Sometimes..."

"They in a plastic package?"

"Usually."

"There you go. Unless the hippy-dippy strawberry farmer made their own plastic with organic resins out back in their eco-friendly petroleum refinery."

"You want to explain without like, being a dick about it?"

He handed me back the open flask, "They're in everything. Man-made synthetics, molecular science type shit. Companies like Nestlé know these things, pay for rigorous studies and research, develop alternatives, test new resources. But, at the end of the day, staying in line with established production stan-dards—a new advertising campaign about healthy living... some broad philanthropy—it's cheaper than the responsible alterna-tive. So, when a new activist group gets all up in arms about recycling code labels... or BPA, these companies develop larger umbrellas for their standards to fit regulation requirements. A little complicity from the FDA, a few donations from various tree-killing special interest groups into the right pockets, and business is allowed to continue as usual. Eventually, the consumer catches on again, and the whole shuffle starts over."

I felt like I wanted to throw up. Whatever I thought I was looking for out here seemed further away than ever. I didn't voice this to the old man, so it caught me off guard when he felt compelled to offer, "Don't worry, kid. It's all a part of something much bigger... you are too."

Gould didn't take his eyes off the road. Rolled the windows down, lit me another smoke. The stagnant night held the heat of the day at street level. It was dark enough by now to hide the tears streaming down my face.

"To keep the honest people out," he said as we creeped past

the empty security vehicle parked outside the rare, stand-alone building with a private parking lot. He took the Dodge around the back of the lot and parked it behind a dumpster enclosure so that we were hidden from view. He killed the engine, opened the driver's door, tossed his lit cig on the ground.

"Wait here," he turned to me before disappearing around the other side of the trash cans. A few seconds later, a security alarm. Gould came running back around the enclosure and jumped into the car.

"What happened," I asked.

He motioned with his hand for me to stay quiet. Time passed in silence, no smoking, no drinking. The police arrived with lights but no sirens. The world around us strobed blue and red as the patrol car circled the lot, ignoring the oasis of shadow behind the enclosure where the Neon so conveniently fit. Standard dispatch chatter droned through the scanner fuzz. The pulsating lights cut off abruptly, and the cruiser pulled out of the lot, back to a regular routine—another couple moments of silence as instructed by Gould. When the city regained its composure, the old man offered the booze again. I drank and handed it back. He finished off what was left.

"Come on," he said.

When we reached the lab's back door, Gould removed what resembled a hotel keycard from the deadbolt, another from the magnetic alarm contact over the jamb. He slipped inside, motioning for me to follow.

The back entrance of the lab led to a white-tiled utility area. Shelves of chemicals and cleaners lined the walls. Sanitary showers on one end. Multiple sinks for different stages of the disinfecting process. I followed Gould through swinging double doors lined with hanging plastic curtains. We entered into a bland hallway: grey floors, grey carpet, grey ceiling tiles. Gould looked like he knew where he was going as we passed offices of various sizes.

The room at the end of the hall was filled with computer workstations. The old man chose one at what could have been random and inserted a thumb drive into the ancient PC tower before booting it up. With a few keystrokes unknown to me, he had admin access and navigated a client database, billing info, requests, and test results. He found a folder he was looking for. Opened it. Scrolled through pages of charts and graphs detailing what I had to believe were water quality test results. The name Nestlé on each page. I caught the words, Lake Arrowhead, saw what looked like an aerial photo of the lake and surrounding area. Gould closed the folder and moved it to his thumb drive.

"It's what you wanted?"

"All there."

"And the chemical levels or whatever, they're high?"

"High enough... not as much as I expected... but high. We got something here, kid."

"Something that'll make a difference this time?"

Gould raised his hand to be quiet. He stared out the open door, down the empty hall. We waited silently for the last few seconds of the transfer. When the progress bar completed, he safe-removed the thumb drive and handed it to me, "You'd better hold onto this."

I meant to ask him why but didn't get the chance. He gestured for me to stay quiet and follow him. We backtracked through the hallway toward the double doors. Gould moved cautiously and, about halfway, stopped altogether. He held up his fist for me to stop. He was staring at the plastic curtain, which could have been swinging decrementally. The fading kinetic energy from our entrance; the first telltale sign of a defect in some airtight filtration ventilation system.

Gould's hand dropped to the revolver inside his suit jacket. The double doors burst open and he pulled the trigger without hesitating.

The revolver echoed off the bland walls.

Each shot less audible than the last as the tiny fibers in my eardrums were obliterated.

The first guy out the door went down, shot in the chest. His dead body slammed into the opposite wall of the narrow hallway, painting the grey with black and red.

The next kept the doorframe to his back, swung a brutal looking shotgun up at us. Gould winged the guy in the leg as the shotgun went off. The guy shot wide, and the drywall around us exploded. I heard the mechanical precision of the shotgun being cocked through the plaster dust. Gould shoved me into the nearest office, opening the door for us with his free hand, firing blindly as we went. The shotgun blasted again.

Gould threw his back against the door, dumped the empty shells from his revolver and slid down to the ground. I sat in a leather chair behind a wooden desk. My chest was on fire, my arm was numb. Blood trickled down my limp right hand, dripped off my fingertips. I forced myself to pull up the right side of my shirt with my left hand.

About a dozen pellets had ripped through my skin.

I could see a piece of my ribs underneath my right breast.

Below that, the tattered welts leaked steady rivulets of blood. I pulled my shirt down, got out my phone. Tapped several times before I got the aim right and cleared the low battery warning. Gould crouched with the side of his face turned to the door. He looked over his shoulder at me, made a face that didn't lift my spirits, and went out into the hall.

*

The hallway tilts under Gould's feet, never flipping or turning but always tipping in one direction so that he has to lean the other way to stay straight. He had been gut shot before, in another life. Had given plenty of blood in search of what felt like purpose on the most lucid days.

Rarely getting answers. Never finding meaning.

He steps over two dead men on his way past the double doors. Bends to retrieve the shotgun, pumps the grip, ejects the spent shell.

A new assailant turns the corner at the far end of the hall. Gould trains the double barrel, adjusting for blood loss, pulls the trigger. Buckshot fills the hallway, pummels his target.

It's hard to take full breaths. His vision clicks on and off. Cold sweat drips from his forehead and down his back. He presses a hand to his lower abdomen where the blood pours out. He fights against the call of unconsciousness, reaching out to join the dead... to rest, promises his work is done.

Voices interrupt the ghost song playing in his head—a whisper from beyond the double doors. A response.

Gould keeps the shotgun low as he shoulders open the swinging doors, pulling the trigger on the upward arc, throwing death around like peanuts.

He yanks the grip and pulls the trigger in rhythm.

Five shells find five lives to take.

Gould coughs and blood comes out. He tosses the shotgun aside. He listens for the next wave of hired grunts but can't hear anything past the ringing in his ears.

*

The door to the office bangs into the wall as Gould crashes through. He slams it shut behind him, falls to his knees.

Blood everywhere.

Jo sits passed out at the desk, iPhone clutched in her fist. The Voice Memo app is open, still recording. Her black hair matted where she pushed it aside with bloodied hands. Skin paler than the usual New England tan.

Gould drags his way to her feet and props himself up against the side of the desk. He reaches up with his free hand—the other keeps the loaded .38 aimed at the door—and pries the phone from Jo's cold grasp. He mashes the buttons on the side until the emergency call alarm goes off. The screen counts down seconds until dialing 911.

The call connects. Gould taps the speakerphone.

"911," comes through the speaker.

Gould wrestles his lips open, tries to reply, but all he can manage is a few blunt vowels gurgled from the dark molasses bile coming up through his esophagus.

"911," the operator repeats, "what's your emergency?"

Gould's lips sputter and twitch.

"If you are experiencing an emergency, please stay on the line. Can you provide your location?"

Exhausted, Gould lets the phone fall away.

The call disconnects. The display returns to normal, filled with missed notifications.

Gould recognizes an Indiana area code on the text preview from the first banner in the list. He inches his arm out, hefts the phone off the ground, spreads spit and blood around the keypad.

Cristine Sheraton: How'd it go? Was he a creep or nah

G: 911

G: 2426 San Fernando 90065

G: Jo is during

G: D

G: Doing

G: DYING

C: ...

C: WTF?!

C: Who is this

G: Her grandfather

2015 Saugus, MA

The RF handheld scanner dings several times in protest when I scan the UPC on a case of water from a stacked pallet.

Dwayne looks over at me, eyes wide in fake surprise.

"You forget how to use that thing?"

"I wish."

"Not in the system?"

"Nah."

"You'd think they'd want new product to sell when it comes in. How it's supposed to do that they don't add it to the fuckin' system?"

"Fuckin'A."

"Don't fuckin'A me, Burke."

"Vendors change so often, they gotta learn to keep up with their own shit."

"Okay. The boss comes down here, you gonna tell him the same thing?"

"Boss isn't coming down here for," I flip the case of water over to read the label, "Sparkling Crystal mineral water."

"Never even heard of that shit."

"Me neither. I get the feeling they'll figure out how to get it sold... what's it matter what I do?"

Dwayne makes the same eyes, but the surprise seemed real, "Jo Burke... did you disappear and go grow yourself some nuts?"

"Why? You need to borrow a pair?"

Dwayne slaps a big palm down on the case of water, "Girl! Wherever you been, you must have lost your damn mind while you were there."

Almost more than that.

I learned to ignore the feeling that someone was outside my door. Down on the landing at the bottom of the stairs. Smoking around the corner of the building in the dusk.

In restless dreams, they didn't wait. Out of body, I could see the faceless killer at the foot of my bed. Backlit by the Blu-ray title screen of *Last Year at Marienbad–Resnais, 1961–Criterion, 2009* playing on a loop. The Me asleep would never know when the final hammer fell.

I ignored the urge to wonder what else there was to know. Ignored the familiar package on the landing at my downstairs neighbor's door. Walked by it without looking three days in a row. I told myself I didn't see it, didn't know the shape. That if I checked the label, I wouldn't recognize the corporate return address from a package I had received months before.

When I finally tore the brown paper off the box, it revealed a 23andme DNA Testing Kit. The label included the return address as I expected, but I wasn't prepared for the name of the recipient: *Rose Amaranth*.

I sprinted up the steps to Maritza's apartment and opened the unlocked door. I grabbed her key ring off the hook without bothering to check if she was around. She only had a few keys on the ring, and I knew which ones I wasn't looking for.

The first-floor apartment had been emptied of everything but the hairballs in the corners of the room and the ADA railings installed on the walls. I noticed the entryway had a small ramp over the threshold for a wheelchair. I brought the opened package inside and set it on the counter separating the kitchen from the living room. An 8x10 photo in an ornate gold frame waited on the counter. A folded piece of notepaper stuck out from one corner.

Jo,
You've inherited the legacy of people who never should have met. There's no proof of our history outside of your blood. You have the chance to escape your heritage, but to do it, you'll have to create your own.
-Love, Victoria Miller Burke (your grandmother)

The framed picture wasn't a photo, but a composite of images from over the years, couples superimposed to appear as if they were together: Joe Sr. and his wife Virginia—my great grandparents. Their son Joe, before he became the man he'd die as. Next to him, a woman in a wheelchair, behind her what appeared to be a younger version of herself, holding Joe by the hand. Beside them, two people I had met but would never know. They hold onto a small girl, no more than three or four years old. She gazes up at her parents with a look I recognized but couldn't recall.

It would take time for me to learn the story of their faces, some features I would never get right. Maybe a scrap of paper wedged in the frame told me all I needed to know. Scribbled hastily, an afterthought torn from the bottom of the notepaper:

You're Family

www.ingramcontent.com/pod-product-compliance
Lightning Source LLC
Chambersburg PA
CBHW060504280326
41933CB00014B/2859